THE
LUCADO

ENCOURAGING
WORD

BIBLE

BY THE BOOK SERIES:
JOHN

MAX LUCADO

GENERAL EDITOR

Thomas Nelson
Since 1798

The Lucado Encouraging Word Bible, John
Copyright © 2020 by Thomas Nelson

Published in Nashville, Tennessee, by Thomas Nelson.
Thomas Nelson is a registered trademark of HarperCollins Christian Publishing, Inc.

Holy Bible, New King James Version, copyright © 1982 by Thomas Nelson.

Library of Congress Control Number: 2021931638

This Bible was set in the Thomas Nelson NKJV Comfort Print Typeface, created at the 2K/DENMARK type foundry.

Printed in the United States of America

21 22 23 24 25 26 27 /TRM/ 12 11 10 9 8 7 6 5 4 3 2 1

BY THE BOOK SERIES

You are holding a single book of the Bible from the *Lucado Encouraging Word Bible*. Even though it is only one book, it certainly does not lack content. This robust edition, which includes interleaved journal pages, offers a compact and portable way to study this special Gospel. It also gives you a taste of what the full *Lucado Encouraging Word Bible* has to offer. If you find your study of John as rewarding as we expect you will, consider obtaining a copy of the full Bible to continue your studies.

Keep in mind that this book is taken in its entirety from the *Lucado Encouraging Word Bible* with no major revisions or deletions. Therefore, it may contain notes and references that point to other parts of the Bible. In addition, some readings may build from previous ones and/or point to others outside of the Book of John. Again, this is simply a taste.

> *Oh, taste and see that the LORD is good;*
> *blessed is the man who trusts in Him!*
>
> Psalm 34:8

BEFORE YOU BEGIN . . .

A WORD FROM MAX LUCADO, GENERAL EDITOR

A discouragement Word conspiracy is afoot. Companies spend billions of dollars to convince us that we are deficient and inadequate. To sell face cream, they tell us that our faces are wrinkled. To sell new clothes, they pronounce that our clothes are out of fashion. To sell hair color, they must persuade us that our hair is dingy. Marketing companies deploy the brightest minds and deepest pockets of our generation to convince us that we are chubby, smelly, ugly, and out-of-date. We are under attack!

We can relate to the two cows grazing in a pasture when a milk truck drove by. On the side of the truck were the words "Pasteurized, homogenized, standardized, vitamin A added." Noticing this, one cow said to the other, "Makes you kind of feel inadequate, doesn't it?"

Inadequacy indwells a billion hearts.

But God has an antidote—His Word. His cure for the weary heart is a fresh dose of truth from the Bible. He is the "God of all comfort" (2 Cor. 1:3). Other translations say *encouragement*.

Jesus encourages us as well. "May our Lord Jesus Christ Himself, and our God and Father . . . comfort your hearts and establish you in every good word and work" (2 Thess. 2:16–17).

When Jesus introduces the Holy Spirit to us in John 14–16, he calls him the *paraklétos*, the noun form of the very word for encouragement.

Scripture encourages us. "For whatever things were written before were written for our learning, that we through the patience and comfort of the Scriptures might have hope" (Rom. 15:4).

The saints in heaven encourage us. "Therefore we also, since we are surrounded by so great a cloud of witnesses, let us lay aside every weight, and the sin which so easily ensnares us, and let us run with endurance the race that is set before us" (Heb. 12:1). A multitude of God's children is urging you on. Like spectators in the stands a crowd of witnesses applauds from the heavens, calling on you to finish strong.

The Father, the Son, the Holy Spirit, the holy Scriptures, the saints. God places a premium on encouragement.

Perhaps you could use some? Life has a way of pulling us under. But God has a way of pulling us up. His way is His word. Let God give you what you need.

Let Him give you His encouraging Word.

INTRODUCTION

The Lucado Encouraging Word Bible is an exhilarating experience. As you read, you'll uncover a saga of suspense and intrigue. Flip over a few pages and find poetry and romance. Turn the pages again and read tales of clashing conquerors, brave shepherds, and a captivating Carpenter. Chronicles of faith, miracles, misdeeds, and good deeds. Kings, queens, peasants—the uncommon and the commonplace. Mystery, suspense, intrigue, drama, humor, poetry, romance . . . it's all in these pages. Stories of real people, with real problems, real joys, and a real Savior. All of that, plus some distinctive features, will help you see that what happened on these pages is still happening today—that the truths of old are truths for our age.

To enrich your study, this Bible has some unique features. These tools will help expand your understanding of Scripture and provide you encouragement in your spiritual journey.

FOR YOUR JOURNEY

You'll notice encouraging devotional notes in the margins. Each of these notes contains a Situation, Observation, Inspiration, and Application section.

The Situation gives a quick look into the context of the chapter; it answers the question, What's going on in this passage?

The Observation goes beneath the action to explain the point of the action: What truth or lesson is noticeable in the action of these people?

The Inspiration takes a point or lesson found in the chapter and amplifies it. Excerpted from the writings of Max Lucado, these inspirations extend the main point and give it a contemporary message that will be useful in your private devotion or for sharing with a group.

The Application brings the message home and helps you ask the right questions: How can I use what I've learned in this chapter? Is there anything about my life that I should change based on what I've learned?

PEOPLE OF THE WORD

Follow the journeys of others from long ago in this feature of nearly one hundred bios of people found or mentioned throughout the Bible. In these articles, you'll see their struggles, triumphs, and God's hand in their lives. These character studies will provide encouragement as you face various circumstances in your life.

"CONSIDER" STUDIES

Throughout the text you will discover Bible studies to help you "consider" various situations you might be confronted with. Use the Articles Index in the front of this Bible to locate specific topics of interest.

JESUS THROUGH THE BIBLE

The Jesus Through the Bible articles are helpful tools for understanding how the Bible truly is one story—the story of God's plan of salvation as fulfilled through His Son, Jesus Christ. These notes help you discover the presence and attributes of Jesus Christ throughout the Old and New Testaments. For example, observe how Jesus is foreshadowed as our High Priest in the Book of Exodus and how His title as Lamb of God can be seen in Leviticus.

—*Karen Davis Hill, Executive Editor for Max Lucado*

PREFACE TO THE
NEW KING JAMES VERSION

To understand the heart behind the New King James Version, one need look no further than the stated intentions of the original King James scholars: "Not to make a new translation . . . but to make a good one better." The New King James Version is a continuation of the labors of the King James translators, unlocking for today's readers the spiritual treasures found especially in the Authorized Version of the Holy Bible.

While seeking to maintain the excellent *form* of the traditional English Bible, special care has also been taken to preserve the work of *precision* which is the legacy of the King James translators.

Where new translation has been necessary, the most complete representation of the original has been rendered by considering the definition and usage of the Hebrew, Aramaic, and Greek words in their contexts. This translation principle, known as *complete equivalence*, seeks to preserve accurately all of the information in the text while presenting it in good literary form.

In addition to accuracy, the translators have also sought to maintain those lyrical and devotional qualities that are so highly regarded in the King James Version. The thought flow and selection of phrases from the King James Version have been preserved wherever possible without sacrificing clarity.

The format of the New King James Version is designed to enhance the vividness, devotional quality, and usefulness of the Bible. Words or phrases in italics indicate expressions in the original language that require clarification by additional English words, as was done in the King James Version. Poetry is structured as verse to reflect the form and beauty of the passage in the original language. The covenant name of God was usually translated from the Hebrew as LORD or GOD, using capital letters as shown, as in the King James Version. This convention is also maintained in the New King James Version when the Old Testament is quoted in the New.

The Hebrew text used for the Old Testament is the 1967/1977 Stuttgart edition of the *Biblia Hebraica*, with frequent comparisons to the Bomberg edition of 1524–25. Ancient versions and the Dead Sea Scrolls were consulted, but the Hebrew is followed wherever possible. Significant variations, explanations, and alternate renderings are mentioned in footnotes.

The Greek text used for the New Testament is the one that was followed by the King James translators: the traditional text of the Greek-speaking churches, called the Received Text or Textus Receptus, first published in 1516. Footnotes indicate significant variants from the Textus Receptus as found in two other editions of the Greek New Testament:

(1) NU-Text: These variations generally represent the Alexandrian or Egyptian text type as found in the critical text published in the twenty-seventh edition of the Nestle-Aland Greek New Testament (N) and in the United Bible Societies' third edition (U).

(2) M-Text: These variations represent readings found in the text of *The Greek New Testament According to the Majority Text*, which follows the consensus of the majority of surviving New Testament manuscripts.

The textual notes in the New King James Version make no evaluation, but objectively present the facts about variant readings.

THE BOOK OF

JOHN

He's an old man, this one who sits on the stool and leans against the wall. Eyes closed and face soft, were it not for his hand stroking his beard, you'd think he was asleep.

Some in the room assume he is. He does this often during worship. As the people sing, his eyes will close and his chin will fall until it rests on his chest, and there he will remain motionless. Silent.

Those who know him well know better. They know he is not resting. He is traveling. Atop the music he journeys back, back, back until he is young again. Strong again. There again. There on the seashore with James and the apostles. There on the trail with the disciples and the women. There in the temple with Caiaphas and the accusers.

It's been sixty years, but John sees Him still. The decades took John's strength, but they didn't take his memory. The years dulled his sight, but they didn't dull his vision. The seasons may have wrinkled his face, but they didn't soften his love.

He had been with God. God had been with him. How could he forget?

The wine that moments before had been water—John could still taste it.

The mud placed on the eyes of the blind man in Jerusalem—John could still remember it.

The aroma of Mary's perfume as it filled the room—John could still smell it.

And the voice. Oh, the voice. His voice. John could still hear it.

I am the light of the world, it rang . . . I am the door . . . I am the way, the truth, the life.

I will come back, it promised, and take you to be with Me.

Those who believe in Me, it assured, will have life even if they die.

AUTHOR:
John, the disciple

DATE WRITTEN:
AD 65–95

KEY THEMES:
• Jesus was and is eternally present in spirit.
• While He was on earth, Jesus communicated with many kinds of people about His mission.
• Jesus performed many miracles to show the nature of His love and power.
• Jesus prepared His followers for the future by promising them the presence of the Holy Spirit.

KEY PEOPLE:
Jesus, John the Baptist, the disciples, Mary Magdalene, Lazarus, Martha, Mary of Bethany

KEY VERSE:
"In the beginning was the Word, and the Word was with God, and the Word was God" (John 1:1).

CONTENTS:

John could hear Him. John could see Him. Scenes branded on his heart. Words seared into his soul. John would never forget. How could he? He had been there.

He opens his eyes and blinks. The singing has stopped. The teaching has begun. John looks at the listeners and listens to the teacher.

If only you could have been there, he thinks.

But he wasn't. Most weren't. Most weren't even born. And most who were there are dead. Peter is. So is James. Nathanael, Martha, Philip. They are all gone. Even Paul, the apostle who came late, is dead.

Only John remains.

He looks again at the church. Small but earnest. They lean forward to hear the teacher. John listens to him. What a task. Speaking of one he never saw. Explaining words he never heard. John is there if the teacher needs him.

But what will happen when John is gone? What will the teacher do then? When John's voice is silent and his tongue stilled? Who will tell them how Jesus silenced the waves? Will they hear how He fed the thousands? Will they remember how He prayed for unity?

How will they know? If only they could have been there.

Suddenly, in His heart he knows what to do.

Later, under the light of a sunlit shaft, the old fisherman unfolds the scroll and begins to write the story of His life . . .

"In the beginning was the Word . . ."

 FOR YOUR JOURNEY

1:1–51

SITUATION

The Greeks and the Jews were familiar with the concept of the word. For the Jews it was an expression of God's wisdom, and for the Greeks it meant reason and intellect.

OBSERVATION

Leaving His heavenly home, Jesus put on human flesh to bring us God's Good News.

INSPIRATION

For John and Andrew, it wasn't enough to listen to John the Baptist. Most would have been content to serve in the shadow of the world's most famous evangelist. Could there be a better teacher? Only one. And when John and Andrew saw

THE ETERNAL WORD

1 In the beginning was the Word, and the Word was with God, and the Word was God. ²He was in the beginning with God. ³All things were made through Him, and without Him nothing was made that was made. ⁴In Him was life, and the life was the light of men. ⁵And the light shines in the darkness, and the darkness did not comprehend[a] it.

JOHN'S WITNESS: THE TRUE LIGHT

⁶There was a man sent from God, whose name *was* John. ⁷This man came for a witness, to bear witness of the Light, that all through him might believe. ⁸He was not that Light, but *was sent* to bear witness of that Light. ⁹That was the true Light which gives light to every man coming into the world.[a]

¹⁰He was in the world, and the world was made through Him, and the world did not know Him. ¹¹He came to His own,[a] and His own[b] did not receive Him. ¹²But as many as received Him, to them He gave the right to become children of God, to those who believe in His name: ¹³who were born, not of blood, nor of the will of the flesh, nor of the will of man, but of God.

1:5 [a] Or *overcome*   1:9 [a] Or *That was the true Light which, coming into the world, gives light to every man.*   1:11 [a] That is, His own things or domain   [b] That is, His own people

THE WORD BECOMES FLESH

14And the Word became flesh and dwelt among us, and we beheld His glory, the glory as of the only begotten of the Father, full of grace and truth.

15John bore witness of Him and cried out, saying, "This was He of whom I said, 'He who comes after me is preferred before me, for He was before me.'"

16And*a* of His fullness we have all received, and grace for grace. 17For the law was given through Moses, *but* grace and truth came through Jesus Christ. 18No one has seen God at any time. The only begotten Son,*a* who is in the bosom of the Father, He has declared *Him*.

A VOICE IN THE WILDERNESS

19Now this is the testimony of John, when the Jews sent priests and Levites from Jerusalem to ask him, "Who are you?"

20He confessed, and did not deny, but confessed, "I am not the Christ."

21And they asked him, "What then? Are you Elijah?"

He said, "I am not."

"Are you the Prophet?"

And he answered, "No."

22Then they said to him, "Who are you, that we may give an answer to those who sent us? What do you say about yourself?"

23He said: "I *am*

'The voice of one crying in the wilderness:
"Make straight the way of the LORD,"'*a*

as the prophet Isaiah said."

24Now those who were sent were from the Pharisees. 25And they asked him, saying, "Why then do you baptize if you are not the Christ, nor Elijah, nor the Prophet?"

26John answered them, saying, "I baptize with water, but there stands One among you whom you do not know. 27It is He who, coming after me, is preferred before me, whose sandal strap I am not worthy to loose."

28These things were done in Bethabara*a* beyond the Jordan, where John was baptizing.

THE LAMB OF GOD

29The next day John saw Jesus coming toward him, and said, "Behold! The Lamb of God who takes away the sin of the world! 30This is He of whom I said, 'After me comes a Man who is preferred before me, for He was before me.' 31I did not know Him; but that He should be revealed to Israel, therefore I came baptizing with water."

32And John bore witness, saying, "I saw the Spirit descending from heaven like a dove, and He remained upon Him. 33I did not know Him, but He who sent me to baptize with water said to me, 'Upon whom you see the Spirit descending, and remaining on Him, this is He who baptizes with the Holy Spirit.' 34And I have seen and testified that this is the Son of God."

1:16*a*NU-Text reads *For.*   1:18*a*NU-Text reads *only begotten God.*
1:23*a*Isaiah 40:3   1:28*a*NU-Text and M-Text read *Bethany.*

Him, they left John the Baptist and followed Jesus. Note the request they made.

"Rabbi," they asked, "where are You staying?" (v. 38). Pretty bold request. They didn't ask Jesus to give them a minute or an opinion or a message or a miracle. They asked for His address. They wanted to hang out with Him. They wanted to know Him. They wanted to know what caused His head to turn and His heart to burn and His soul to yearn. They wanted to study His eyes and follow His steps. They wanted to see Him. They wanted to know what made Him laugh and if He ever got tired.

And most of all, they wanted to know, *Could Jesus be who John said He was—and if He is, what on earth is God doing on the earth?* You can't answer such a question by talking to His cousin; you've got to talk to the Man Himself.

Jesus' answer to the disciples? "Come and see" (v. 39). He didn't say, "Come and glance" or "Come and peek." He said, "Come and see." Bring your bifocals and binoculars. There is no time for side-glances or occasional peeks. "Looking unto Jesus, the author and finisher of our faith" (Heb. 12:2).

The disciple fixes his eyes on the Savior.

APPLICATION
If people want to know what God is like, they can look at Jesus. If they want to know what Jesus is like, they should be able to look at His followers. Can people see Christ in you?

THE FIRST DISCIPLES

³⁵Again, the next day, John stood with two of his disciples. ³⁶And looking at Jesus as He walked, he said, "Behold the Lamb of God!"

³⁷The two disciples heard him speak, and they followed Jesus. ³⁸Then Jesus turned, and seeing them following, said to them, "What do you seek?"

They said to Him, "Rabbi" (which is to say, when translated, Teacher), "where are You staying?"

³⁹He said to them, "Come and see." They came and saw where He was staying, and remained with Him that day (now it was about the tenth hour).

⁴⁰One of the two who heard John *speak,* and followed Him,

NATHANAEL

When Philip breathlessly gushed, "We have found Him of whom Moses in the law, and also the prophets, wrote—" (John 1:45), Nathanael was incredulous. When Philip added that this messianic One was Jesus *of Nazareth,* Nathanael didn't even try to hide his cynicism. How could Israel's great Savior-King ever come from a sketchy place like that?

Philip's reply was the perfect answer for anyone with doubts about Jesus: "Come and see" (1:46).

Come. In other words, don't just scoff from a distance. Draw near. Take the initiative to investigate the radical claims of Jesus. If they aren't true, you merely lose a little time and effort. If they are true, however, nothing in the universe is more important.

See. Don't blindly follow the opinions of the crowd. Open your eyes, your mind, and your heart. Resist the foolish pride that vows, *Even if I'm confronted with strong evidence that undermines my skepticism about Jesus, I will not alter my stance.* On the contrary, leave behind your preconceived notions about God and faith. Look with fresh eyes at the words and works of Christ.

Nathanael accepted Philip's challenge. He went and saw firsthand. He approached Jesus humbly and honestly. Before long,

this man of integrity found himself gawking at Jesus and admitting, "You are the son of God! You are the King of Israel!" (1:49).

After two thousand years, "Come and see" is still the best advice for doubters (which, let's face it, is all of the people some of the time and some of the people all of the time).

Draw near. Observe. See the broken who are being made whole? See the guilty living in freedom? See the bitter being filled with forgiveness and love?

The more we pay attention to Jesus, the more we watch how He works in and through His followers, the more reasons we find to believe His astounding claims.

"Come and see" is the glad invitation to every skeptic in every era. It's the encouraging word before we even get to the good news that Jesus will never reject a seeker, and He will never run away from your doubts or hard questions.

was Andrew, Simon Peter's brother. ⁴¹He first found his own brother Simon, and said to him, "We have found the Messiah" (which is translated, the Christ). ⁴²And he brought him to Jesus.

Now when Jesus looked at him, He said, "You are Simon the son of Jonah.ᵃ You shall be called Cephas" (which is translated, A Stone).

PHILIP AND NATHANAEL

⁴³The following day Jesus wanted to go to Galilee, and He found Philip and said to him, "Follow Me." ⁴⁴Now Philip was from Bethsaida, the city of Andrew and Peter. ⁴⁵Philip found Nathanael and said to him, "We have found Him of whom Moses in the law, and also the prophets, wrote—Jesus of Nazareth, the son of Joseph."

⁴⁶And Nathanael said to him, "Can anything good come out of Nazareth?"

Philip said to him, "Come and see."

⁴⁷Jesus saw Nathanael coming toward Him, and said of him, "Behold, an Israelite indeed, in whom is no deceit!"

⁴⁸Nathanael said to Him, "How do You know me?"

1:42 ᵃ NU-Text reads *John*.

ANDREW

Despite being one of Christ's twelve hand-picked disciples, Andrew is mentioned only twelve times in the New Testament. Unlike his louder, better known brother, Peter, we never see Andrew preaching to the masses, writing epistles, or being freed from prison by angels. If Andrew participated in healings or other miracles, those wonders took place in the shadows, not in the limelight.

And yet, even if most wouldn't consider Andrew a giant in the faith, there's no debating the giant role he played in God's kingdom. Thanks to John the Baptist, Andrew met Jesus and received an invitation to spend the afternoon with Him. By the day's end Andrew was convinced.

He left, and the Bible says, "The first thing Andrew did was to find his brother Simon and tell him, 'We have found the Messiah' (that is, the Christ). And he brought him to Jesus. Jesus looked at him and said, 'You are Simon son of John. You will be called

Cephas' (which, when translated, is Peter)" (John 1:41–42 NIV).

If it weren't for Andrew, the world might never have heard of Peter! Perhaps Simon would have spent the remainder of his days checking his fishing nets instead of changing the world.

Andrew was more tortoise than hare, more bread crust than crème brûlée. He faithfully followed Jesus, quietly using his gift for *connection*. He connected others to Christ (see 12:20–22). He connected available resources with urgent needs (see 6:8–9). He connected eternal truth to everyday life (see Mark 13:3–4). No fanfare, just faithfulness.

2:1–25

SITUATION

Weddings were an important part of Jewish culture. An entire village or town often participated in the festivities. Jesus performed His first miracle at this wedding in Cana.

OBSERVATION

Jesus is concerned about us because we are His children and His friends.

INSPIRATION

Picture six men walking on a narrow road.

The men's faces are eager, but common. Their leader is confident, but unknown. They call Him Rabbi.

Where are they going? They haven't been told, but they each have their own idea.

Then a chorus of confusion breaks out and ends only when Jesus lifts His hand and says softly, "We're on our way to a wedding."

"Why would we go to a wedding?"

The answer? It's found in the second verse of John 2. "Jesus and His disciples were invited to the wedding."

Big deal? I think so. I think it's significant that common folk in a little town enjoyed being with Jesus. Jesus was a likable fellow. And His disciples should be the same. I'm not talking debauchery, drunkenness, and adultery. I'm not endorsing compromise, coarseness, or obscenity. I am simply crusading for the freedom to enjoy a good joke, enliven a dull party, and appreciate a fun evening.

APPLICATION

How long has it been since you had a good laugh? A hilarious time of fun with Christian friends? Jesus wants us to rejoice and enjoy life. Celebrate!

Jesus answered and said to him, "Before Philip called you, when you were under the fig tree, I saw you."

⁴⁹Nathanael answered and said to Him, "Rabbi, You are the Son of God! You are the King of Israel!"

⁵⁰Jesus answered and said to him, "Because I said to you, 'I saw you under the fig tree,' do you believe? You will see greater things than these." ⁵¹And He said to him, "Most assuredly, I say to you, hereafter^a you shall see heaven open, and the angels of God ascending and descending upon the Son of Man."

WATER TURNED TO WINE

2 On the third day there was a wedding in Cana of Galilee, and the mother of Jesus was there. ²Now both Jesus and His disciples were invited to the wedding. ³And when they ran out of wine, the mother of Jesus said to Him, "They have no wine."

⁴Jesus said to her, "Woman, what does your concern have to do with Me? My hour has not yet come."

⁵His mother said to the servants, "Whatever He says to you, do *it.*"

⁶Now there were set there six waterpots of stone, according to the manner of purification of the Jews, containing twenty or thirty gallons apiece. ⁷Jesus said to them, "Fill the waterpots with water." And they filled them up to the brim. ⁸And He said to them, "Draw *some* out now, and take *it* to the master of the feast." And they took *it.* ⁹When the master of the feast had tasted the water that was made wine, and did not know where it came from (but the servants who had drawn the water knew), the master of the feast called the bridegroom. ¹⁰And he said to him, "Every man at the beginning sets out the good wine, and when the *guests* have well drunk, then the inferior. You have kept the good wine until now!"

¹¹This beginning of signs Jesus did in Cana of Galilee, and manifested His glory; and His disciples believed in Him.

¹²After this He went down to Capernaum, He, His mother, His brothers, and His disciples; and they did not stay there many days.

JESUS CLEANSES THE TEMPLE

¹³Now the Passover of the Jews was at hand, and Jesus went up to Jerusalem. ¹⁴And He found in the temple those who sold oxen and sheep and doves, and the money changers doing business. ¹⁵When He had made a whip of cords, He drove them all out of the temple, with the sheep and the oxen, and poured out the changers' money and overturned the tables. ¹⁶And He said to those who sold doves, "Take these things away! Do not make My Father's house a house of merchandise!" ¹⁷Then His disciples remembered that it was written, "Zeal for Your house has eaten^a Me up."^b

¹⁸So the Jews answered and said to Him, "What sign do You show to us, since You do these things?"

¹⁹Jesus answered and said to them, "Destroy this temple, and in three days I will raise it up."

²⁰Then the Jews said, "It has taken forty-six years to build this temple, and will You raise it up in three days?"

1:51^aNU-Text omits *hereafter.*   2:17^aNU-Text and M-Text read *will eat.*
^bPsalm 69:9

21But He was speaking of the temple of His body. 22Therefore, when He had risen from the dead, His disciples remembered that He had said this to them;[a] and they believed the Scripture and the word which Jesus had said.

THE DISCERNER OF HEARTS

23Now when He was in Jerusalem at the Passover, during the feast, many believed in His name when they saw the signs which He did. 24But Jesus did not commit Himself to them, because He knew all *men*, 25and had no need that anyone should testify of man, for He knew what was in man.

THE NEW BIRTH

3 There was a man of the Pharisees named Nicodemus, a ruler of the Jews. 2This man came to Jesus by night and said to Him, "Rabbi, we know that You are a teacher come from God; for no one can do these signs that You do unless God is with him."

3Jesus answered and said to him, "Most assuredly, I say to you, unless one is born again, he cannot see the kingdom of God."

4Nicodemus said to Him, "How can a man be born when he is old? Can he enter a second time into his mother's womb and be born?"

5Jesus answered, "Most assuredly, I say to you, unless one is born of water and the Spirit, he cannot enter the kingdom of God. 6That which is born of the flesh is flesh, and that which is born of the Spirit is spirit. 7Do not marvel that I said to you, 'You must be born again.' 8The wind blows where it wishes, and you hear the sound of it, but cannot tell where it comes from and where it goes. So is everyone who is born of the Spirit."

9Nicodemus answered and said to Him, "How can these things be?"

10Jesus answered and said to him, "Are you the teacher of Israel, and do not know these things? 11Most assuredly, I say to you, We speak what We know and testify what We have seen, and you do not receive Our witness. 12If I have told you earthly things and you do not believe, how will you believe if I tell you heavenly things? 13No one has ascended to heaven but He who came down from heaven, *that is,* the Son of Man who is in heaven.[a] 14And as Moses lifted up the serpent in the wilderness, even so must the Son of Man be lifted up, 15that whoever believes in Him should not perish but[a] have eternal life. 16For God so loved the world that He gave His only begotten Son, that whoever believes in Him should not perish but have everlasting life. 17For God did not send His Son into the world to condemn the world, but that the world through Him might be saved.

18"He who believes in Him is not condemned; but he who does not believe is condemned already, because he has not believed in the name of the only begotten Son of God. 19And this is the condemnation, that the light has come into the world, and men loved darkness rather than light, because their deeds were evil. 20For everyone practicing evil hates the light and does not come to the light, lest his deeds should be exposed. 21But he

---

2:22 [a] NU-Text and M-Text omit *to them.*   3:13 [a] NU-Text omits *who is in heaven.*   3:15 [a] NU-Text omits *not perish but.*

FOR YOUR JOURNEY

3:1–36

SITUATION
Nicodemus belonged to the highest governing body of the Jewish people, the Sanhedrin. Many of these Jewish leaders were bound by tradition and legalism.

OBSERVATION
Jesus came to free men and women from slavery to sin and from the chains of legalism.

INSPIRATION
The meeting between Jesus and Nicodemus was more than an encounter between two religious figures. It was a collision between two philosophies. Two opposing views on salvation.

Nicodemus thought the person did the work; Jesus says God does the work.

These two views encompass all views. All the world religions can be placed in one of two camps: legalism or grace.

A legalist believes the supreme force behind salvation is you. If you look right, speak right, and belong to the right segment of the right group, you will be saved. The brunt of responsibility doesn't lie with God; it lies within you.

Spirituality, Jesus says, comes not from church attendance or good deeds or correct doctrine, but from heaven itself. Such words must have set Nicodemus back on his heels. But Jesus was just getting started.

Salvation is God's business. Grace is His idea, His work, and His expense. He offers it to whom He desires, when He desires. Our job in the process is to inform the people, not screen the people.

The question must have been written all over Nicodemus's face. Why would God do this? What would motivate Him to offer such a gift? What Jesus

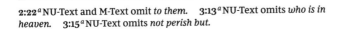

told Nicodemus, Nicodemus could never have imagined. The motive behind the gift of new birth? Love. "For God so loved the world that He gave His only begotten Son, that whoever believes in Him should not perish but have everlasting life" (v. 16).

Nicodemus has never heard such words. Never. He has had many discussions of salvation. But this is the first in which no rules were given. No system was offered. No code or ritual.

who does the truth comes to the light, that his deeds may be clearly seen, that they have been done in God."

JOHN THE BAPTIST EXALTS CHRIST

22After these things Jesus and His disciples came into the land of Judea, and there He remained with them and baptized. 23Now John also was baptizing in Aenon near Salim, because there was much water there. And they came and were baptized. 24For John had not yet been thrown into prison.

25Then there arose a dispute between *some* of John's disciples and the Jews about purification. 26And they came to John and said to him, "Rabbi, He who was with you beyond the Jordan, to whom you have testified—behold, He is baptizing, and all are coming to Him!"

NICODEMUS

When we first meet this distinguished Pharisee in John 3, Nicodemus is clearly intrigued by the miracle-working teacher from Galilee. But as a member of the Sanhedrin, Judaism's most powerful ruling council, Nicodemus has to be careful. He can't act too supportive of this controversial rabbi, so he calls on Him secretly at night.

Nicodemus indicates he wants to discuss religious matters, but Jesus cuts right to the chase. No small talk. Straight to the point. Straight to the heart. Straight to the problem. "Most assuredly, I say to you, unless one is born again, he cannot see the kingdom of God" (John 3:3).

The tongue-tied scholar mumbles a couple questions to which Jesus essentially replies, "Nicodemus, you know God's Word—but you need His Spirit. You need rebirth, not rules and rituals. The life you long for comes through trusting, not trying harder."

Then, when Jesus declares, "For God so loved the world that He gave His only begotten Son, that whoever believes in Him should not perish but have everlasting life" (3:16), Nicodemus doesn't say another word. He's too deep in thought, too busy wrestling with a truth that's tantalizing . . . and troubling.

Nicodemus reappears in John 7. There the Jewish religious leaders are raking Jesus over the coals. To everyone's surprise—perhaps even his own—Nicodemus blurts out, "Does our law judge a man before it hears him and knows what he is doing?" (7:51). The comment, while not exactly a ringing endorsement, is somewhat sympathetic. As you might guess, it isn't well received. But it raises a question: Is Nicodemus having a change of heart?

In John 19, we encounter Nicodemus for a third and final time. He's with another well-known, highly respected religious leader, Joseph of Arimathea. What are they doing? They're giving the bruised and broken body of Jesus a decent burial. God only knows what this act of kindness cost them professionally and socially.

The New Testament doesn't overtly say it, but the evidence strongly suggests that Nicodemus came to faith. Sometime between the days of first listening to Jesus and finally laying Him in the grave, Nicodemus believed. He was born again.

27John answered and said, "A man can receive nothing unless it has been given to him from heaven. 28You yourselves bear me witness, that I said, 'I am not the Christ,' but, 'I have been sent before Him.' 29He who has the bride is the bridegroom; but the friend of the bridegroom, who stands and hears him, rejoices greatly because of the bridegroom's voice. Therefore this joy of mine is fulfilled. 30He must increase, but I *must* decrease. 31He who comes from above is above all; he who is of the earth is earthly and speaks of the earth. He who comes from heaven is above all. 32And what He has seen and heard, that He testifies; and no one receives His testimony. 33He who has received His testimony has certified that God is true. 34For He whom God has sent speaks the words of God, for God does not give the Spirit by measure. 35The Father loves the Son, and has given all things into His hand. 36He who believes in the Son has everlasting life; and he who does not believe the Son shall not see life, but the wrath of God abides on him."

A SAMARITAN WOMAN MEETS HER MESSIAH

4 Therefore, when the Lord knew that the Pharisees had heard that Jesus made and baptized more disciples than John 2(though Jesus Himself did not baptize, but His disciples), 3He left Judea and departed again to Galilee. 4But He needed to go through Samaria.

5So He came to a city of Samaria which is called Sychar, near the plot of ground that Jacob gave to his son Joseph. 6Now

"Everyone who believes can have eternal life in Him," Jesus told him. Could God be so generous?

APPLICATION
Are there religious "rules" you observe but do not understand? Did God command them, or did mere people create them? Do they help you feel close to God? If so, keep them. Are some confusing to you? Ask your pastor to explain them to you.

 FOR YOUR JOURNEY

4:1–54
SITUATION
Although the Jews did not like the Samaritans, Jesus purposely went through their territory. His disciples were amazed to find Jesus talking with a Samaritan— especially a woman!

 Jesus Through the Bible

Jesus: Whoever Believes

The word *whoever* unfurls John 3:16 as a banner for the ages. *Whoever* unrolls the welcome mat of heaven to humanity. *Whoever* invites the world to God. Jesus could have so easily narrowed the scope, changing *whoever* into *whatever*. "Whatever Jew believes" or "Whatever woman follows Me." But He used no qualifier. The pronoun is wonderfully indefinite. After all, who isn't a *whoever*?

The word sledgehammers racial fences and dynamites social classes. It bypasses gender borders and surpasses ancient traditions. *Whoever* makes it clear: God exports His grace worldwide. For those who attempt to restrict it, Jesus has a word: *Whoever*.
- "Whoever confesses Me before men, him I will also confess before My Father who is in heaven" (Matt. 10:32).
- "Whoever finds their life will lose it, and whoever loses their life for my sake will find it" (Matt. 10:39 NIV).
- "Whoever does the will of God is My brother and My sister and mother" (Mark 3:35).

- "Whoever believes and is baptized will be saved, but whoever does not believe will be condemned" (Mark 16:16 NIV).
- "Whoever believes in the Son has eternal life, but whoever rejects the Son will not see life, for God's wrath remains on them" (John 3:36 NIV).
- "Whoever drinks of the water that I shall give him will never thirst" (John 4:14).
- "Whoever comes to me I will never drive away" (John 6:37 NIV).
- "Whoever lives and believes in Me shall never die" (John 11:26).
- "Whoever desires, let him take the water of life freely" (Rev. 22:17).

Titus 2:11 assures us that "the grace of God has appeared to all men." And Paul contends that Jesus Christ "gave himself as a ransom for all people" (1 Tim. 2:6 NIV). Peter affirms that God is "not willing that any should perish but that all should come to repentance" (2 Pet. 3:9). God's gospel has a "whoever" policy.

For more on Jesus Through the Bible, see Jesus: The Resurrection and the Life.

OBSERVATION

Jesus knows everything about us before we tell Him.

INSPIRATION

Remarkable. It wasn't within the colonnades of a Roman court that He announced His identity.

No, it was in the shade of a well in a rejected land to an ostracized woman. His eyes must have danced as He whispered the secret.

"I am the Messiah."

Don't miss the drama of the moment. Look at her eyes, wide with amazement. Listen to her as she struggles for words. "Y-y-y-you a-a-a-are the M-m-m-messiah!"

Suddenly the insignificance of her life was swallowed by the significance of the moment. "God is here! God has come! God cares . . . for me!"

That is why she grabbed the first person she saw and announced her discovery, "I just talked to a man who knows everything I ever did . . . and He loves me anyway!"

The disciples offered Jesus some food. He refused it—He was too excited! He had just done what He does best. He had taken a life that was drifting and given it direction.

He was exuberant!

APPLICATION

What doubts and misgivings about Jesus do you have that hinder your faith? First, realize that even the disciples doubted, right up to the end (see Matt. 28:17). Second, commit your doubts to the Lord, and ask for faith to live for Christ. Third, have confidence in Jesus the living Word. He will refresh your faith.

Jacob's well was there. Jesus therefore, being wearied from *His* journey, sat thus by the well. It was about the sixth hour.

⁷A woman of Samaria came to draw water. Jesus said to her, "Give Me a drink." ⁸For His disciples had gone away into the city to buy food.

⁹Then the woman of Samaria said to Him, "How is it that You, being a Jew, ask a drink from me, a Samaritan woman?" For Jews have no dealings with Samaritans.

¹⁰Jesus answered and said to her, "If you knew the gift of God, and who it is who says to you, 'Give Me a drink,' you would have asked Him, and He would have given you living water."

¹¹The woman said to Him, "Sir, You have nothing to draw with, and the well is deep. Where then do You get that living water? ¹²Are You greater than our father Jacob, who gave us the well, and drank from it himself, as well as his sons and his livestock?"

¹³Jesus answered and said to her, "Whoever drinks of this water will thirst again, ¹⁴but whoever drinks of the water that I shall give him will never thirst. But the water that I shall give him will become in him a fountain of water springing up into everlasting life."

¹⁵The woman said to Him, "Sir, give me this water, that I may not thirst, nor come here to draw."

¹⁶Jesus said to her, "Go, call your husband, and come here."

¹⁷The woman answered and said, "I have no husband."

Jesus said to her, "You have well said, 'I have no husband,' ¹⁸for you have had five husbands, and the one whom you now have is not your husband; in that you spoke truly."

¹⁹The woman said to Him, "Sir, I perceive that You are a prophet. ²⁰Our fathers worshiped on this mountain, and you *Jews* say that in Jerusalem is the place where one ought to worship."

²¹Jesus said to her, "Woman, believe Me, the hour is coming when you will neither on this mountain, nor in Jerusalem, worship the Father. ²²You worship what you do not know; we know what we worship, for salvation is of the Jews. ²³But the hour is coming, and now is, when the true worshipers will worship the Father in spirit and truth; for the Father is seeking such to worship Him. ²⁴God *is* Spirit, and those who worship Him must worship in spirit and truth."

²⁵The woman said to Him, "I know that Messiah is coming" (who is called Christ). "When He comes, He will tell us all things."

²⁶Jesus said to her, "I who speak to you am *He.*"

THE WHITENED HARVEST

²⁷And at this *point* His disciples came, and they marveled that He talked with a woman; yet no one said, "What do You seek?" or, "Why are You talking with her?"

²⁸The woman then left her waterpot, went her way into the city, and said to the men, ²⁹"Come, see a Man who told me all things that I ever did. Could this be the Christ?" ³⁰Then they went out of the city and came to Him.

³¹In the meantime His disciples urged Him, saying, "Rabbi, eat."

³²But He said to them, "I have food to eat of which you do not know."

33Therefore the disciples said to one another, "Has anyone brought Him *anything* to eat?"

34Jesus said to them, "My food is to do the will of Him who sent Me, and to finish His work. 35Do you not say, 'There are still four months and *then* comes the harvest'? Behold, I say to you, lift up your eyes and look at the fields, for they are already white for harvest! 36And he who reaps receives wages, and gathers fruit for eternal life, that both he who sows and he who reaps may rejoice together. 37For in this the saying is true: 'One sows and another reaps.' 38I sent you to reap that for which you have not labored; others have labored, and you have entered into their labors."

THE WOMAN AT THE WELL

The last thing she'd wanted was to see anyone, which is why she always fetched water in the hottest part of the day. But when she got to Jacob's well, a man was there, slumped wearily against the stones. A stranger. Obviously Jewish.

She waited for Him to scowl, scramble to His feet, make some derogatory comment about Samaritans like her, and walk away. Only He didn't. When He politely asked her for a drink, her jaw dropped in shock—and her water pot nearly did too.

Smiling at her reaction, the man said something like, "Actually, come to think of it, you're the one who should be asking Me for drink. I could give you *living* water."

It was all so unexpected, so strange. It was like He could see straight into her parched soul. Sense exactly how she felt. Like a dried-up pond in July, her heart felt cracked and broken, her hope evaporating by the day, her life slowly leaking away.

When He started rattling off the intimate details of her checkered romantic history, it all clicked. *Of course, He's a prophet.* She felt embarrassed, even though nothing about the stranger's tone or demeanor was harsh.

She tried clumsily to change the subject. He wouldn't let her. Without the slightest hint of condemnation, He kept bringing the conversation back around to her dehydrated soul. "I can make it so you'll never thirst again," He promised. "And I can even turn your heart into a fountain that refreshes others." The more He talked, the more she sensed something welling up inside her. His words seemed to her like a gushing river. She wanted to drink them in and swim in them forever.

And so the woman ran eagerly back to town to find the very neighbors who typically went out of their way to avoid her. "Come, see a Man who told me all things that I ever did," she shouted. "Could this be the Christ?" (John 4:29).

They did come and see. "And many of the Samaritans of that city believed in Him because of the word of the woman" (4:39).

Are you thirsty today? Are you weary of solutions that only leave you more parched than before?

The offer still stands: Come to Jesus. Take a drink. Become a river of life.

5:1-47

SITUATION
While He was traveling to Jerusalem to attend the Feast of the Passover, Jesus made a detour to Bethesda to meet the needs of the people.

OBSERVATION
Jesus had special concern for the suffering and the neglected.

INSPIRATION
Jesse spotted Meagan through the window of a café, squeezing lemon into her glass of water. For a couple of minutes he watched. The restaurant had a retro look, a throwback to diner days with soda counters and silver-rimmed tables. Two men in an adjacent booth said something to her; she ignored them. A server offered her a menu; she declined it. A car screeched to a stop and honked at a jaywalking pedestrian; she looked up. That's when Meagan saw him.

Jesse smiled. She didn't. But neither did she turn away. She watched him cross the narrow street, enter the café, and walk toward her booth. He asked if he could join her, and she nodded. As he signaled the server, Meagan noticed Jesse looked tired.

He said little as he waited on his coffee. She spoke even less, at first. But once she began, her whole story tumbled out. Dropped by a boyfriend in Missouri. Fed up with her family. Someone told her she could make fast money in commercials. She escaped to the West Coast. Audition after audition. Rejection after rejection. Finally cosmetics school. "I never even finished," she confessed. "I heard about the opening at Bentley Bishop's. Went for an interview and . . ."—she looked away—"after doing what he wanted, he hired me. And now"—a tear bubbled—"I'm here. I pay the rent and don't go hungry. Twenty-one years old

THE SAVIOR OF THE WORLD

39And many of the Samaritans of that city believed in Him because of the word of the woman who testified, "He told me all that I *ever* did." 40So when the Samaritans had come to Him, they urged Him to stay with them; and He stayed there two days. 41And many more believed because of His own word.

42Then they said to the woman, "Now we believe, not because of what you said, for we ourselves have heard *Him* and we know that this is indeed the Christ,ᵃ the Savior of the world."

WELCOME AT GALILEE

43Now after the two days He departed from there and went to Galilee. 44For Jesus Himself testified that a prophet has no honor in his own country. 45So when He came to Galilee, the Galileans received Him, having seen all the things He did in Jerusalem at the feast; for they also had gone to the feast.

A NOBLEMAN'S SON HEALED

46So Jesus came again to Cana of Galilee where He had made the water wine. And there was a certain nobleman whose son was sick at Capernaum. 47When he heard that Jesus had come out of Judea into Galilee, he went to Him and implored Him to come down and heal his son, for he was at the point of death. 48Then Jesus said to him, "Unless you *people* see signs and wonders, you will by no means believe."

49The nobleman said to Him, "Sir, come down before my child dies!"

50Jesus said to him, "Go your way; your son lives." So the man believed the word that Jesus spoke to him, and he went his way. 51And as he was now going down, his servants met him and told *him,* saying, "Your son lives!"

52Then he inquired of them the hour when he got better. And they said to him, "Yesterday at the seventh hour the fever left him." 53So the father knew that *it was* at the same hour in which Jesus said to him, "Your son lives." And he himself believed, and his whole household.

54This again *is* the second sign Jesus did when He had come out of Judea into Galilee.

A MAN HEALED AT THE POOL OF BETHESDA

5 After this there was a feast of the Jews, and Jesus went up to Jerusalem. 2Now there is in Jerusalem by the Sheep *Gate* a pool, which is called in Hebrew, Bethesda,ᵃ having five porches. 3In these lay a great multitude of sick people, blind, lame, paralyzed, waiting for the moving of the water. 4For an angel went down at a certain time into the pool and stirred up the water; then whoever stepped in first, after the stirring of the water, was made well of whatever disease he had.ᵃ 5Now a certain man was there who had an infirmity thirty-eight years. 6When Jesus saw him lying there, and knew that he already had been *in that condition* a long time, He said to him, "Do you want to be made well?"

4:42ᵃNU-Text omits *the Christ.* 5:2ᵃNU-Text reads *Bethzatha.*
5:4ᵃNU-Text omits *waiting for the moving of the water* at the end of verse 3, and all of verse 4.

It's called Bethesda. It could be called Central Park, Metropolitan Hospital, or even Joe's Bar and Grill. It could be the homeless huddled beneath a downtown overpass. It could be Calvary Baptist. It could be any collection of hurting people.

An underwater spring caused the pool to bubble occasionally. The people believed the bubbles were caused by the dipping of angels' wings. They also believed that the first person to touch the water after the angel did would be healed. Did healing occur? I don't know. But I do know crowds of invalids came to give it a try.

Picture a battleground strewn with wounded bodies, and you see Bethesda. Imagine a nursing home overcrowded and understaffed, and you see the pool. Call to mind the orphans in Bangladesh or the abandoned in New Delhi, and you will see what people saw when they passed Bethesda. As they passed, what did they hear? An endless wave of groans. What did they witness? A field of faceless need. What did they do? Most walked past, ignoring the people.

But not Jesus. He is in Jerusalem for a feast. He is alone. He is not there to teach the disciples or to draw a crowd. The people need Him—so He's there.

Can you picture it? Jesus walking among the suffering.

What is He thinking? When an infected hand touches His ankle, what does He do? When a blind child stumbles in Jesus' path, does He reach down to catch the child? When a wrinkled hand extends for alms, how does Jesus respond?

Whether the watering hole is Bethesda or Bill's Bar, how does God feel when people hurt?

It's worth the telling of the story if all we do is watch Him walk. It's worth it just to know He even came. He didn't have to, you know. Surely there are more sanitary crowds in Jerusalem. Surely there are more enjoyable activities. After all, this is the Feast of the Passover. It's an exciting time in the holy city. People have come from miles around to meet God in the temple.

Little do they know that God is with the sick.

Little do they know that God is walking slowly, stepping carefully between the beggars and the blind.

Little do they know that the strong young carpenter who surveys the ragged landscape of pain is God.

STUDY GUIDE
READ JOHN 5:1–15.

- Think of a time when a friend showed special concern for you during a difficult time in your life. How did that person's support help you?

- What do you think motivated Jesus to go to Bethesda during a celebration?

- What do Jesus' actions in this story teach us about His character?

- What are some of the challenges of ministering to people with a serious illness? What are the rewards?

- How can we demonstrate God's love to people who are suffering?

- Why is it important for believers to minister to hurting people?

- Think of someone you know who is hurting. How can you reach out to that person?

- How can the church become more sensitive to the suffering around it?

and surviving L.A. Sounds like the chorus of a country-western song. But I'm okay. At least that's what I tell myself."

Jesse's sandwich arrived. He offered her half, but she declined. After a couple of bites, he wiped his mouth with a napkin.

"Meagan, I know you. I've watched you stain pillows with tears and walk streets because you couldn't sleep. I know you. And I know you hate who you are becoming."

"So"—Meagan touched the corner of her eye with the back of a knuckle—"if you're such a psychic, tell me: where's God in all this? I've been looking for Him a long, long time." With a sudden increase in volume, she began listing misdeeds on her fingers. "I ran out on my folks. I sleep with my boss. I've spent more time on a barstool than a church pew. I'm tired, tired of it all." She bit her lip and looked away.

Jesse inclined the same direction and caught her attention. She looked up to see him beaming, energetic, as though he were an algebra professor and she was struggling with two plus two.

"Where is God in all this?" He repeated her question. "Nearer than you've ever dreamed." He took her glass and held it. "Meagan, everyone who drinks this water will get thirsty again. But I offer a different drink. Anyone who drinks the water I give will never thirst. Not ever."

Again, silence.

With a finger Meagan bounced the ice cubes in the glass. Finally she asked, "Never?"

"Not ever."

She looked away, then looked back, and, with every ounce of honesty she owned, asked, "Tell me, Jesse. Who in the world are you?"

Her new friend leaned forward in response and replied, "I thought you'd never ask."

7The sick man answered Him, "Sir, I have no man to put me into the pool when the water is stirred up; but while I am coming, another steps down before me."

8Jesus said to him, "Rise, take up your bed and walk." 9And immediately the man was made well, took up his bed, and walked.

And that day was the Sabbath. 10The Jews therefore said to him who was cured, "It is the Sabbath; it is not lawful for you to carry your bed."

11He answered them, "He who made me well said to me, 'Take up your bed and walk.'"

12Then they asked him, "Who is the Man who said to you, 'Take up your bed and walk'?" 13But the one who was healed did not know who it was, for Jesus had withdrawn, a multitude being in *that* place. 14Afterward Jesus found him in the temple, and said to him, "See, you have been made well. Sin no more, lest a worse thing come upon you."

15The man departed and told the Jews that it was Jesus who had made him well.

HONOR THE FATHER AND THE SON

16For this reason the Jews persecuted Jesus, and sought to kill Him,[a] because He had done these things on the Sabbath. 17But Jesus answered them, "My Father has been working until now, and I have been working."

18Therefore the Jews sought all the more to kill Him, because He not only broke the Sabbath, but also said that God was His Father, making Himself equal with God. 19Then Jesus answered and said to them, "Most assuredly, I say to you, the Son can do nothing of Himself, but what He sees the Father do; for whatever He does, the Son also does in like manner. 20For the Father loves the Son, and shows Him all things that He Himself does; and He will show Him greater works than these, that you may marvel. 21For as the Father raises the dead and gives life to *them,* even so the Son gives life to whom He will. 22For the Father judges no one, but has committed all judgment to the Son, 23that all should honor the Son just as they honor the Father. He who does not honor the Son does not honor the Father who sent Him.

LIFE AND JUDGMENT ARE THROUGH THE SON

24"Most assuredly, I say to you, he who hears My word and believes in Him who sent Me has everlasting life, and shall not come into judgment, but has passed from death into life. 25Most assuredly, I say to you, the hour is coming, and now is, when the dead will hear the voice of the Son of God; and those who hear will live. 26For as the Father has life in Himself, so He has granted the Son to have life in Himself, 27and has given Him authority to execute judgment also, because He is the Son of Man. 28Do not marvel at this; for the hour is coming in which all who are in the graves will hear His voice 29and come forth— those who have done good, to the resurrection of life, and those who have done evil, to the resurrection of condemnation. 30I can of Myself do nothing. As I hear, I judge; and My judgment

---

5:16 [a] NU-Text omits *and sought to kill Him.*

is righteous, because I do not seek My own will but the will of the Father who sent Me.

THE FOURFOLD WITNESS

31"If I bear witness of Myself, My witness is not true. 32There is another who bears witness of Me, and I know that the witness which He witnesses of Me is true. 33You have sent to John, and he has borne witness to the truth. 34Yet I do not receive testimony from man, but I say these things that you may be saved. 35He was the burning and shining lamp, and you were willing for a time to rejoice in his light. 36But I have a greater witness than John's; for the works which the Father has given Me to finish—the very works that I do—bear witness of Me, that the Father has sent Me. 37And the Father Himself, who sent Me, has testified of Me. You have neither heard His voice at any time, nor seen His form. 38But you do not have His word abiding in you, because whom He sent, Him you do not believe. 39You search the Scriptures, for in them you think you have eternal life; and these are they which testify of Me. 40But you are not willing to come to Me that you may have life.

41"I do not receive honor from men. 42But I know you, that you do not have the love of God in you. 43I have come in My Father's name, and you do not receive Me; if another comes in his own name, him you will receive. 44How can you believe, who receive honor from one another, and do not seek the honor that *comes* from the only God? 45Do not think that I shall accuse you to the Father; there is *one* who accuses you—Moses, in whom you trust. 46For if you believed Moses, you would believe Me; for he wrote about Me. 47But if you do not believe his writings, how will you believe My words?"

FEEDING THE FIVE THOUSAND

6 After these things Jesus went over the Sea of Galilee, which is *the Sea* of Tiberias. 2Then a great multitude followed Him, because they saw His signs which He performed on those who were diseased. 3And Jesus went up on the mountain, and there He sat with His disciples.

4Now the Passover, a feast of the Jews, was near. 5Then Jesus lifted up *His* eyes, and seeing a great multitude coming toward Him, He said to Philip, "Where shall we buy bread, that these may eat?" 6But this He said to test him, for He Himself knew what He would do.

7Philip answered Him, "Two hundred denarii worth of bread is not sufficient for them, that every one of them may have a little."

8One of His disciples, Andrew, Simon Peter's brother, said to Him, 9"There is a lad here who has five barley loaves and two small fish, but what are they among so many?"

10Then Jesus said, "Make the people sit down." Now there was much grass in the place. So the men sat down, in number about five thousand. 11And Jesus took the loaves, and when He had given thanks He distributed *them* to the disciples, and the disciples*ᵃ* to those sitting down; and likewise of the fish, as much as they wanted. 12So when they were filled, He said to His disciples,

---

6:11 *ᵃ* NU-Text omits *to the disciples, and the disciples.*

The dimensions of God's love are different too. You've lived a life in a house of imperfect love. You think God is going to cut you as the coach did, or abandon you as your father did, or judge you as false religion did, or curse you as your friend did. He won't, but it takes time to be convinced.

For that reason, abide in Him. Hang on to Christ the same way a branch clutches the vine. According to Jesus, the branch models His definition of *abiding*. "As the branch cannot bear fruit

"Gather up the fragments that remain, so that nothing is lost." ¹³Therefore they gathered *them* up, and filled twelve baskets with the fragments of the five barley loaves which were left over by those who had eaten. ¹⁴Then those men, when they had seen the sign that Jesus did, said, "This is truly the Prophet who is to come into the world."

JESUS WALKS ON THE SEA

¹⁵Therefore when Jesus perceived that they were about to come and take Him by force to make Him king, He departed again to the mountain by Himself alone.

¹⁶Now when evening came, His disciples went down to the sea, ¹⁷got into the boat, and went over the sea toward Capernaum. And it was already dark, and Jesus had not come to them. ¹⁸Then the sea arose because a great wind was blowing. ¹⁹So

CONSIDER: *GOD'S PRESENCE*

Their question: What hope do we have of surviving a stormy night?

My question: Where is God when His world is stormy?

Doubt-storms: turbulent days when the enemy is too big, the task too great, the future too bleak, and the answers too few.

Every so often a storm will come, and I'll look up into the blackening sky and say, "God, a little light, please?"

The light came for the disciples. A figure came to them walking on the water. It wasn't what they expected. Perhaps they were looking for angels to descend or heaven to open. Maybe they were listening for a divine proclamation to still the storm. We don't know what they were looking for. But one thing is for sure, they weren't looking for Jesus to come walking on the water. And since Jesus came in a way they didn't expect, they almost missed seeing the answer to their prayers.

And unless we look, and listen closely, we risk making the same mistake. God's lights in our dark nights are as numerous as the stars, if only we'll look for them.

When Jesus comes, the disciples in the boat may have thought, *He'll split the sky. The sea will be calm. The clouds will disperse.*

When God comes, we doubters think, *all pain will flee. Life will be tranquil. No questions will remain.*

And because we look for the bonfire, we miss the candle. Because we listen for the shout, we miss the whisper.

But it is in burnished candles that God comes, and through whispered promises He speaks: "When you doubt, look around; I am closer than you think."

STUDY GUIDE
READ JOHN 6:16–21.

- What are the tough questions we face when we're dealing with doubt?

- Describe a time when God has come to you or someone you know in a time of darkness.

- On what do we base our expectations of how God will help us?

- When Jesus walked on the water, why do you think Peter wanted to go to Jesus on the water rather than asking Jesus to come to him?

- How do you think faith enables miracles such as Peter standing on water?

- After having witnessed Jesus' power and miracles, why do you think the disciples were still amazed when He worked a miracle?

- What kinds of things make you doubt God?

- What are your expectations of how God will meet you in life?

when they had rowed about three or four miles,[a] they saw Jesus walking on the sea and drawing near the boat; and they were afraid. 20But He said to them, "It is I; do not be afraid." 21Then they willingly received Him into the boat, and immediately the boat was at the land where they were going.

THE BREAD FROM HEAVEN

22On the following day, when the people who were standing on the other side of the sea saw that there was no other boat there, except that one which His disciples had entered,[a] and that Jesus had not entered the boat with His disciples, but His disciples had gone away alone— 23however, other boats came from Tiberias, near the place where they ate bread after the Lord had given thanks— 24when the people therefore saw that Jesus was not there, nor His disciples, they also got into boats and came to Capernaum, seeking Jesus. 25And when they found Him on the other side of the sea, they said to Him, "Rabbi, when did You come here?"

26Jesus answered them and said, "Most assuredly, I say to you, you seek Me, not because you saw the signs, but because you ate of the loaves and were filled. 27Do not labor for the food which perishes, but for the food which endures to everlasting life, which the Son of Man will give you, because God the Father has set His seal on Him."

28Then they said to Him, "What shall we do, that we may work the works of God?"

29Jesus answered and said to them, "This is the work of God, that you believe in Him whom He sent."

30Therefore they said to Him, "What sign will You perform then, that we may see it and believe You? What work will You do? 31Our fathers ate the manna in the desert; as it is written, 'He gave them bread from heaven to eat.'"[a]

32Then Jesus said to them, "Most assuredly, I say to you, Moses did not give you the bread from heaven, but My Father gives you the true bread from heaven. 33For the bread of God is He who comes down from heaven and gives life to the world."

34Then they said to Him, "Lord, give us this bread always."

35And Jesus said to them, "I am the bread of life. He who comes to Me shall never hunger, and he who believes in Me shall never thirst. 36But I said to you that you have seen Me and yet do not believe. 37All that the Father gives Me will come to Me, and the one who comes to Me I will by no means cast out. 38For I have come down from heaven, not to do My own will, but the will of Him who sent Me. 39This is the will of the Father who sent Me, that of all He has given Me I should lose nothing, but should raise it up at the last day. 40And this is the will of Him who sent Me, that everyone who sees the Son and believes in Him may have everlasting life; and I will raise him up at the last day."

REJECTED BY HIS OWN

41The Jews then complained about Him, because He said, "I am the bread which came down from heaven." 42And they said,

of itself, unless it abides in the vine, neither can you, unless you abide in Me" (John 15:4).

Does a branch ever release the vine? Only at the risk of death. Does the branch ever stop eating? Nope. It receives nutrients twenty-four hours a day. Would you say the branch is vine-dependent? I would. If branches had seminars, the topic would be "Get a Grip: Secrets of Vine Grabbing." But branches don't have seminars because attendance requires releasing the vine, something they refuse to do.

How well do you pass the vine test? Do you ever release yourself from Christ's love? Go unnourished? Do you ever stop drinking from His reservoir? Do so at the certain risk of a parched heart.

APPLICATION
What is the source of your spiritual nourishment? Movies, television, or music? Do you need to change your diet so that Christ becomes the strong force in your life? Do this by Bible reading, prayer, and worship.

6:19[a] Literally *twenty-five or thirty stadia*   6:22[a] NU-Text omits *that* and *which His disciples had entered.*   6:31[a] Exodus 16:4; Nehemiah 9:15; Psalm 78:24

"Is not this Jesus, the son of Joseph, whose father and mother we know? How is it then that He says, 'I have come down from heaven'?"

43Jesus therefore answered and said to them, "Do not murmur among yourselves. 44No one can come to Me unless the Father who sent Me draws him; and I will raise him up at the last day. 45It is written in the prophets, 'And they shall all be taught by God.'a Therefore everyone who has heard and learnedb from the Father comes to Me. 46Not that anyone has seen the Father, except He who is from God; He has seen the Father. 47Most assuredly, I say to you, he who believes in Mea has everlasting life. 48I am the bread of life. 49Your fathers ate the manna in the wilderness, and are dead. 50This is the bread which comes down from heaven, that one may eat of it and not die. 51I am the living bread which came down from heaven. If anyone eats of this bread, he will live forever; and the bread that I shall give is My flesh, which I shall give for the life of the world."

52The Jews therefore quarreled among themselves, saying, "How can this Man give us His flesh to eat?"

53Then Jesus said to them, "Most assuredly, I say to you, unless you eat the flesh of the Son of Man and drink His blood, you have no life in you. 54Whoever eats My flesh and drinks My blood has eternal life, and I will raise him up at the last day. 55For My flesh is food indeed,a and My blood is drink indeed. 56He who eats My flesh and drinks My blood abides in Me, and I in him. 57As the living Father sent Me, and I live because of the Father, so he who feeds on Me will live because of Me. 58This is the bread which came down from heaven—not as your fathers ate the manna, and are dead. He who eats this bread will live forever."

59These things He said in the synagogue as He taught in Capernaum.

MANY DISCIPLES TURN AWAY

60Therefore many of His disciples, when they heard this, said, "This is a hard saying; who can understand it?"

61When Jesus knew in Himself that His disciples complained about this, He said to them, "Does this offend you? 62What then if you should see the Son of Man ascend where He was before? 63It is the Spirit who gives life; the flesh profits nothing. The words that I speak to you are spirit, and they are life. 64But there are some of you who do not believe." For Jesus knew from the beginning who they were who did not believe, and who would betray Him. 65And He said, "Therefore I have said to you that no one can come to Me unless it has been granted to him by My Father."

66From that time many of His disciples went back and walked with Him no more. 67Then Jesus said to the twelve, "Do you also want to go away?"

68But Simon Peter answered Him, "Lord, to whom shall we go? You have the words of eternal life. 69Also we have come to believe and know that You are the Christ, the Son of the living God."a

70Jesus answered them, "Did I not choose you, the twelve,

6:45 aIsaiah 54:13   bM-Text reads hears and has learned.   6:47 aNU-Text omits in Me.   6:55 aNU-Text reads true food and true drink.   6:69 aNU-Text reads You are the Holy One of God.

and one of you is a devil?" ⁷¹He spoke of Judas Iscariot, *the son* of Simon, for it was he who would betray Him, being one of the twelve.

JESUS' BROTHERS DISBELIEVE

7 After these things Jesus walked in Galilee; for He did not want to walk in Judea, because the Jews*ᵃ* sought to kill Him. ²Now the Jews' Feast of Tabernacles was at hand. ³His brothers therefore said to Him, "Depart from here and go into Judea, that Your disciples also may see the works that You are doing. ⁴For no one does anything in secret while he himself seeks to be known openly. If You do these things, show Yourself to the world." ⁵For even His brothers did not believe in Him.

⁶Then Jesus said to them, "My time has not yet come, but your time is always ready. ⁷The world cannot hate you, but it hates Me because I testify of it that its works are evil. ⁸You go up to this feast. I am not yet*ᵃ* going up to this feast, for My time has not yet fully come." ⁹When He had said these things to them, He remained in Galilee.

THE HEAVENLY SCHOLAR

¹⁰But when His brothers had gone up, then He also went up to the feast, not openly, but as it were in secret. ¹¹Then the Jews sought Him at the feast, and said, "Where is He?" ¹²And there was much complaining among the people concerning Him. Some said, "He is good"; others said, "No, on the contrary, He deceives the people." ¹³However, no one spoke openly of Him for fear of the Jews.

¹⁴Now about the middle of the feast Jesus went up into the temple and taught. ¹⁵And the Jews marveled, saying, "How does this Man know letters, having never studied?"

¹⁶Jesus*ᵃ* answered them and said, "My doctrine is not Mine, but His who sent Me. ¹⁷If anyone wills to do His will, he shall know concerning the doctrine, whether it is from God or *whether* I speak on My own *authority.* ¹⁸He who speaks from himself seeks his own glory; but He who seeks the glory of the One who sent Him is true, and no unrighteousness is in Him. ¹⁹Did not Moses give you the law, yet none of you keeps the law? Why do you seek to kill Me?"

²⁰The people answered and said, "You have a demon. Who is seeking to kill You?"

²¹Jesus answered and said to them, "I did one work, and you all marvel. ²²Moses therefore gave you circumcision (not that it is from Moses, but from the fathers), and you circumcise a man on the Sabbath. ²³If a man receives circumcision on the Sabbath, so that the law of Moses should not be broken, are you angry with Me because I made a man completely well on the Sabbath? ²⁴Do not judge according to appearance, but judge with righteous judgment."

COULD THIS BE THE CHRIST?

²⁵Now some of them from Jerusalem said, "Is this not He whom they seek to kill? ²⁶But look! He speaks boldly, and they

---

7:1*ᵃ*That is, the ruling authorities   7:8*ᵃ*NU-Text omits *yet.*   7:16*ᵃ*NU-Text and M-Text read *So Jesus.*

FOR YOUR JOURNEY

7:1-53

SITUATION
Jesus prepared His followers for His death, and the leading priests and Pharisees became more determined than ever to arrest Him.

OBSERVATION
Jesus knows how it feels to be persecuted and threatened. His own family did not believe in Him. But Jesus never wavered from His mission to bring the water of life to thirsty souls.

INSPIRATION
Where do you find water for the soul? Jesus gave an answer one October day in Jerusalem. People had packed the streets for the annual reenactment of the rock-giving-water miracle of Moses. In honor of their nomadic ancestors, they slept in tents. In tribute to the desert stream, they poured out water. Each morning a priest filled a golden pitcher with water from the Gihon spring and carried it down a people-lined path to the temple. Announced by trumpets, the priest encircled the altar with a libation of liquid. He did this every day, once a day, for seven days. Then on the last day, the great day, the priest gave the altar a Jericho loop—seven circles—dousing it with seven vessels of water. It may have been at this very moment that the rustic rabbi from the northlands commanded the people's attention. "On the last day, that great day of the feast, Jesus *stood and cried out*, saying, 'If anyone thirsts, let him come to Me and drink. He who believes in Me, as the Scripture has said, out of his heart will flow rivers of living water'" (vv. 37–38, emphasis added).

Finely frocked priests turned. Surprised people looked. Wide-eyed children and toothless grandparents paused. They knew this man. Some had heard Him preach in the Hebrew hills;

others, in the city streets. Two and a half years had passed since He'd emerged from the Jordan waters. The crowd had seen this carpenter before.

But had they seen Him this intense? He stood up and shouted. The traditional rabbinic teaching posture was sitting and speaking. But Jesus stood up and shouted out. The blind man shouted, appealing for sight (see Mark 10:46–47); the sinking Peter shouted, begging for help (see Matt. 14:29–30); and the demon-possessed man shouted, pleading for mercy (see Mark 5:2–7). John uses the same Greek verb to portray the volume of Jesus' voice. Forget a kind clearing of the throat. God was pounding His gavel on heaven's bench. Christ demanded attention.

He shouted because His time was short. The sand in the neck of His hourglass was down to measurable grains. In six months He'd be dragging a cross through these streets. And the people? The people thirsted. They needed water, not for their throats, but for their hearts. So Jesus invited: *Are your insides starting to shrivel? Drink Me.*

APPLICATION
Does Jesus have a slot in your schedule? Do you plan your day around your time with Him, or does He get whatever time is left? Your spiritual life will dry up if you don't continue to drink the water of life. Give Jesus priority by praying often and by making decisions you believe He would make.

say nothing to Him. Do the rulers know indeed that this is truly[a] the Christ? 27However, we know where this Man is from; but when the Christ comes, no one knows where He is from."

28Then Jesus cried out, as He taught in the temple, saying, "You both know Me, and you know where I am from; and I have not come of Myself, but He who sent Me is true, whom you do not know. 29But[a] I know Him, for I am from Him, and He sent Me."

30Therefore they sought to take Him; but no one laid a hand on Him, because His hour had not yet come. 31And many of the people believed in Him, and said, "When the Christ comes, will He do more signs than these which this *Man* has done?"

JESUS AND THE RELIGIOUS LEADERS
32The Pharisees heard the crowd murmuring these things concerning Him, and the Pharisees and the chief priests sent officers to take Him. 33Then Jesus said to them,[a] "I shall be with you a little while longer, and *then* I go to Him who sent Me. 34You will seek Me and not find *Me,* and where I am you cannot come."

35Then the Jews said among themselves, "Where does He intend to go that we shall not find Him? Does He intend to go to the Dispersion among the Greeks and teach the Greeks? 36What is this thing that He said, 'You will seek Me and not find Me, and where I am you cannot come'?"

THE PROMISE OF THE HOLY SPIRIT
37On the last day, that great *day* of the feast, Jesus stood and cried out, saying, "If anyone thirsts, let him come to Me and drink. 38He who believes in Me, as the Scripture has said, out of his heart will flow rivers of living water." 39But this He spoke concerning the Spirit, whom those believing[a] in Him would receive; for the Holy[b] Spirit was not yet *given,* because Jesus was not yet glorified.

WHO IS HE?
40Therefore many[a] from the crowd, when they heard this saying, said, "Truly this is the Prophet." 41Others said, "This is the Christ."

But some said, "Will the Christ come out of Galilee? 42Has not the Scripture said that the Christ comes from the seed of David and from the town of Bethlehem, where David was?" 43So there was a division among the people because of Him. 44Now some of them wanted to take Him, but no one laid hands on Him.

REJECTED BY THE AUTHORITIES
45Then the officers came to the chief priests and Pharisees, who said to them, "Why have you not brought Him?"

46The officers answered, "No man ever spoke like this Man!"

47Then the Pharisees answered them, "Are you also deceived? 48Have any of the rulers or the Pharisees believed in Him? 49But this crowd that does not know the law is accursed."

7:26[a]NU-Text omits *truly.*   7:29[a]NU-Text and M-Text omit *But.*
7:33[a]NU-Text and M-Text omit *to them.*   7:39[a]NU-Text reads *who believed.*
[b]NU-Text omits *Holy.*   7:40[a]NU-Text reads *some.*

⁵⁰Nicodemus (he who came to Jesus by night,ᵃ being one of them) said to them, ⁵¹"Does our law judge a man before it hears him and knows what he is doing?"

⁵²They answered and said to him, "Are you also from Galilee? Search and look, for no prophet has arisenᵃ out of Galilee."

AN ADULTERESS FACES THE LIGHT OF THE WORLD

⁵³And everyone went to his *own* house.ᵃ

8 But Jesus went to the Mount of Olives. ²Now earlyᵃ in the morning He came again into the temple, and all the people came to Him; and He sat down and taught them. ³Then the scribes and Pharisees brought to Him a woman caught in adultery. And when they had set her in the midst, ⁴they said to Him, "Teacher, this woman was caughtᵃ in adultery, in the very act. ⁵Now Moses, in the law, commandedᵃ us that such should be stoned.ᵇ But what do You say?"ᶜ ⁶This they said, testing Him, that they might have *something* of which to accuse Him. But Jesus stooped down and wrote on the ground with *His* finger, as though He did not hear.ᵃ

⁷So when they continued asking Him, He raised Himself upᵃ and said to them, "He who is without sin among you, let him throw a stone at her first." ⁸And again He stooped down and wrote on the ground. ⁹Then those who heard *it,* being convicted by *their* conscience,ᵃ went out one by one, beginning with the oldest *even* to the last. And Jesus was left alone, and the woman standing in the midst. ¹⁰When Jesus had raised Himself up and saw no one but the woman, He said to her,ᵃ "Woman, where are those accusers of yours?ᵇ Has no one condemned you?"

¹¹She said, "No one, Lord."

And Jesus said to her, "Neither do I condemn you; go andᵃ sin no more."

¹²Then Jesus spoke to them again, saying, "I am the light of the world. He who follows Me shall not walk in darkness, but have the light of life."

JESUS DEFENDS HIS SELF-WITNESS

¹³The Pharisees therefore said to Him, "You bear witness of Yourself; Your witness is not true."

¹⁴Jesus answered and said to them, "Even if I bear witness of Myself, My witness is true, for I know where I came from and where I am going; but you do not know where I come from and where I am going. ¹⁵You judge according to the flesh; I judge no one. ¹⁶And yet if I do judge, My judgment is true; for I am not alone, but I *am* with the Father who sent Me. ¹⁷It is also written in your law that the testimony of two men is true. ¹⁸I am One

---

7:50ᵃNU-Text reads *before.*   7:52ᵃNU-Text reads *is to rise.*   7:53ᵃThe words *And everyone* through *sin no more* (8:11) are bracketed by NU-Text as not original. They are present in over 900 manuscripts.   8:2ᵃM-Text reads *very early.*   8:4ᵃM-Text reads *we found this woman.*   8:5ᵃM-Text reads *in our law Moses commanded.*   ᵇNU-Text and M-Text read *to stone such.*   ᶜM-Text adds *about her.*   8:6ᵃNU-Text and M-Text omit *as though He did not hear.* 8:7ᵃM-Text reads *He looked up.*   8:9ᵃNU-Text and M-Text omit *being convicted by their conscience.*   8:10ᵃNU-Text omits *and saw no one but the woman;* M-Text reads *He saw her and said.*   ᵇNU-Text and M-Text omit *of yours.*   8:11ᵃNU-Text and M-Text add *from now on.*

FOR YOUR JOURNEY

8:1-59

SITUATION
Jesus convinced the Pharisees that God could forgive the most hideous sins. He also tried to convince them of His divine lineage, but they assumed He was demon-possessed or mad. The Pharisees grew angry when Jesus told them that they had fallen out of favor with God.

OBSERVATION
We must seek God's wisdom to overcome difficult situations in life.

INSPIRATION
Sightless and heartless redeemers. That's not the Redeemer of the New Testament.

Compare the blind Christ of the Redeemer statue in Rio de Janeiro to the compassionate one seen by a frightened woman early one morning in Jerusalem.

Jesus sits surrounded by a horseshoe of listeners. Some nod their heads in agreement and open their hearts in obedience.

We don't know His topic that morning. Prayer, perhaps. Or maybe kindness or anxiety. But whatever it was, it was soon interrupted when people burst into the courtyard.

The listeners scramble to get out of the way. The mob is made up of religious leaders, the elders and deacons of their day. And struggling to keep her balance on the crest of this angry wave is a scantily-clad woman.

Only moments before she had been in bed with a man who was not her husband. Was this how she made her living? Maybe. Maybe not. We don't know.

But we do know that a door was jerked open, and she was yanked from a bed.

And now, with holy strides, the mob storms toward the teacher. They throw the woman in His direction.

"We found this woman in bed with a man!" cries the leader. "The Law says to stone her. What do you say?"

The accusers are persistent. "Tell us, teacher! What do you want us to do with her?"

He just raised His head and offered an invitation, "I guess if you've never made a mistake, then you have a right to stone this woman." He looked back down and began to draw on the earth again.

Someone cleared his throat as if to speak, but no one spoke. Feet shuffled. Eyes dropped. Then thud . . . thud . . . thud . . . rocks fell to the ground. The men walked away. They came as one, but they left one by one.

Jesus told the woman to look up. "Is there no one to condemn you?"

Maybe she expected Him to scold her. I'm not sure, but I do know this: What she got, she never expected. She got a promise and a commission.

The promise: "Then neither do I condemn you."

The commission: "Go and sin no more."

The woman turns and walks into anonymity. But we can be confident of one thing: On that morning in Jerusalem, she saw Jesus and Jesus saw her. And could we somehow transport her to Rio de Janeiro and let her stand at the base of the *Crist Redentor*, I know what her response would be.

"That's not the Jesus I saw," she would say. For the Jesus she saw didn't have a hard heart. And the Jesus that saw her didn't have blind eyes.

However, if we could somehow transport her to Calvary and let her stand at the base of the cross, you know what she would say. "That's Him."

She would recognize His voice. It's raspier and weaker, but the

who bears witness of Myself, and the Father who sent Me bears witness of Me."

¹⁹Then they said to Him, "Where is Your Father?"

Jesus answered, "You know neither Me nor My Father. If you had known Me, you would have known My Father also."

²⁰These words Jesus spoke in the treasury, as He taught in the temple; and no one laid hands on Him, for His hour had not yet come.

JESUS PREDICTS HIS DEPARTURE

²¹Then Jesus said to them again, "I am going away, and you will seek Me, and will die in your sin. Where I go you cannot come."

²²So the Jews said, "Will He kill Himself, because He says, 'Where I go you cannot come'?"

²³And He said to them, "You are from beneath; I am from above. You are of this world; I am not of this world. ²⁴Therefore I said to you that you will die in your sins; for if you do not believe that I am *He,* you will die in your sins."

²⁵Then they said to Him, "Who are You?"

And Jesus said to them, "Just what I have been saying to you from the beginning. ²⁶I have many things to say and to judge concerning you, but He who sent Me is true; and I speak to the world those things which I heard from Him."

²⁷They did not understand that He spoke to them of the Father.

²⁸Then Jesus said to them, "When you lift up the Son of Man, then you will know that I am *He,* and *that* I do nothing of Myself; but as My Father taught Me, I speak these things. ²⁹And He who sent Me is with Me. The Father has not left Me alone, for I always do those things that please Him." ³⁰As He spoke these words, many believed in Him.

THE TRUTH SHALL MAKE YOU FREE

³¹Then Jesus said to those Jews who believed Him, "If you abide in My word, you are My disciples indeed. ³²And you shall know the truth, and the truth shall make you free."

³³They answered Him, "We are Abraham's descendants, and have never been in bondage to anyone. How *can* You say, 'You will be made free'?"

³⁴Jesus answered them, "Most assuredly, I say to you, whoever commits sin is a slave of sin. ³⁵And a slave does not abide in the house forever, *but* a son abides forever. ³⁶Therefore if the Son makes you free, you shall be free indeed.

ABRAHAM'S SEED AND SATAN'S

³⁷"I know that you are Abraham's descendants, but you seek to kill Me, because My word has no place in you. ³⁸I speak what I have seen with My Father, and you do what you have seen with*ᵃ* your father."

³⁹They answered and said to Him, "Abraham is our father."

Jesus said to them, "If you were Abraham's children, you would do the works of Abraham. ⁴⁰But now you seek to kill Me, a Man who has told you the truth which I heard from God. Abraham did not do this. ⁴¹You do the deeds of your father."

8:38*ᵃ*NU-Text reads *heard from.*

Then they said to Him, "We were not born of fornication; we have one Father—God."

[42]Jesus said to them, "If God were your Father, you would love Me, for I proceeded forth and came from God; nor have I come of Myself, but He sent Me. [43]Why do you not understand My speech? Because you are not able to listen to My word. [44]You are of *your* father the devil, and the desires of your father you want to do. He was a murderer from the beginning, and does not stand in the truth, because there is no truth in him. When he speaks a lie, he speaks from his own *resources,* for he is a liar and the father of it. [45]But because I tell the truth, you do not believe Me. [46]Which of you convicts Me of sin? And if I tell the truth, why do you not believe Me? [47]He who is of God hears God's words; therefore you do not hear, because you are not of God."

BEFORE ABRAHAM WAS, I AM

[48]Then the Jews answered and said to Him, "Do we not say rightly that You are a Samaritan and have a demon?"

[49]Jesus answered, "I do not have a demon; but I honor My Father, and you dishonor Me. [50]And I do not seek My *own* glory; there is One who seeks and judges. [51]Most assuredly, I say to you, if anyone keeps My word he shall never see death."

[52]Then the Jews said to Him, "Now we know that You have a demon! Abraham is dead, and the prophets; and You say, 'If anyone keeps My word he shall never taste death.' [53]Are You greater than our father Abraham, who is dead? And the prophets are dead. Who do You make Yourself out to be?"

[54]Jesus answered, "If I honor Myself, My honor is nothing. It is My Father who honors Me, of whom you say that He is your[a] God. [55]Yet you have not known Him, but I know Him. And if I say, 'I do not know Him,' I shall be a liar like you; but I do know Him and keep His word. [56]Your father Abraham rejoiced to see My day, and he saw *it* and was glad."

[57]Then the Jews said to Him, "You are not yet fifty years old, and have You seen Abraham?"

[58]Jesus said to them, "Most assuredly, I say to you, before Abraham was, I AM."

[59]Then they took up stones to throw at Him; but Jesus hid Himself and went out of the temple,[a] going through the midst of them, and so passed by.

A MAN BORN BLIND RECEIVES SIGHT

9 Now as *Jesus* passed by, He saw a man who was blind from birth. [2]And His disciples asked Him, saying, "Rabbi, who sinned, this man or his parents, that he was born blind?"

[3]Jesus answered, "Neither this man nor his parents sinned, but that the works of God should be revealed in him. [4]I[a] must work the works of Him who sent Me while it is day; *the* night is coming when no one can work. [5]As long as I am in the world, I am the light of the world."

[6]When He had said these things, He spat on the ground and made clay with the saliva; and He anointed the eyes of the blind man with the clay. [7]And He said to him, "Go, wash in the pool

words are the same, "Father, forgive them." And she would recognize His eyes. Eyes that saw her not as she was, but as she was intended to be.

APPLICATION
Discerning right from wrong is sometimes easy, sometimes hard. How about those who have made the wrong choice? How do you judge people? Seek God's wisdom so that you are slow to condemn and quick to show compassion.

FOR YOUR JOURNEY

9:1–41

SITUATION
Jesus restored sight to a man born blind. The Pharisees questioned the man but refused to believe that Jesus had healed him. Despite the obvious evidence, the scoffing Pharisees threw the healed man out of the temple.

OBSERVATION
Some people doubt Christ's work, not for lack of evidence but because they don't want to believe it. Jesus' mission is often missed by the "wise" people of this world.

INSPIRATION
Born blind only to be healed. Healed only to be kicked out. Kicked out only to be left alone. The peak of Everest and the heat of Sahara, all in one Sabbath. Now he can't even beg anymore. How would that feel?

You may know all too well. I know of a man who has buried four children. A single mother in our church is raising two autistic sons. We buried a neighbor whose cancer led to heart trouble, which created pneumonia. Her health record was as thick as a phone book. Do some people seem to be dealt more than their share of bad hands?

If so, Jesus knows. He knows how they feel, and he knows

8:54[a]NU-Text and M-Text read *our.* 8:59[a]NU-Text omits the rest of this verse. 9:4[a]NU-Text reads *We.*

where they are. "Jesus heard that they had cast him out; and . . . found him" (v. 35). In case the stable birth wasn't enough. If three decades of earth walking and miracle working are insufficient. If there be any doubt regarding God's full-bore devotion, He does things like this. He tracks down a troubled pauper.

The beggar lifts his eyes to look into the face of the One who started all this. Is he going to criticize Christ? Complain to Christ? You couldn't blame him

of Siloam" (which is translated, Sent). So he went and washed, and came back seeing.

8Therefore the neighbors and those who previously had seen that he was blind*a* said, "Is not this he who sat and begged?" 9Some said, "This is he." Others *said,* "He is like him."*a* He said, "I am *he.*"

10Therefore they said to him, "How were your eyes opened?" 11He answered and said, "A Man called Jesus made clay and anointed my eyes and said to me, 'Go to the pool of*a* Siloam and wash.' So I went and washed, and I received sight." 12Then they said to him, "Where is He?" He said, "I do not know."

9:8*a* NU-Text reads *a beggar.*   9:9*a* NU-Text reads *"No, but he is like him."* 9:11*a* NU-Text omits *the pool of.*

CONSIDER: *USEFULNESS*

Why do you think he's blind?" one asked.

"He must have sinned."

"No, it's his folks' fault."

"Jesus, what do You think? Why is he blind?"

"He's blind to show what God can do."

The apostles knew what was coming; they had seen this look in Jesus' eyes before. They knew what He was going to do, but they didn't know how He was going to do it. Lightning? Thunder? A shout? A clap of the hands? They all watched.

Jesus began to work His mouth a little. The onlookers stared. "What is He doing?" He moved His jaw as if He were chewing on something.

Some of the people began to get restless. Jesus just chewed. His jaw rotated around until He had what He wanted. Spit. Ordinary saliva.

If no one said it, somebody had to be thinking it: *Yuck!*

Jesus spat on the ground, stuck His finger into the puddle, and stirred. Soon it was a mud pie, and He smeared some of the mud across the blind man's eyes.

The same One who'd turned a stick into a scepter and a pebble into a missile now turned saliva and mud into a balm for the blind.

Once again the mundane became majestic. Once again the dull became divine, the humdrum holy. Once again God's power was seen, not through the ability of the instrument, but through its availability.

"Blessed are the meek," Jesus explained. Blessed are the available. Blessed are the conduits, the tunnels, the tools. Deliriously joyful are the ones who believe that if God has used sticks, rocks, and spit to do His will, then He can use us.

STUDY GUIDE
READ JOHN 9:1–12.

- Why do you think Jesus chose to heal that way?

- If you had witnessed this event, how do you think you would have responded?

- Describe a time when you have witnessed God using something unlikely to accomplish His will.

- Think about your personal strengths and weaknesses. How has God worked through your weaknesses for His glory?

- When have you seen a person's weakness or even a specific disability used for God's glory?

- What does it feel like to be used by God?

- Put into your own words why the "availability" of an instrument is just as or even more important than the "ability."

- In what ways can you be more available to God?

THE PHARISEES EXCOMMUNICATE THE HEALED MAN

13They brought him who formerly was blind to the Pharisees. 14Now it was a Sabbath when Jesus made the clay and opened his eyes. 15Then the Pharisees also asked him again how he had received his sight. He said to them, "He put clay on my eyes, and I washed, and I see."

16Therefore some of the Pharisees said, "This Man is not from God, because He does not keep the Sabbath."

Others said, "How can a man who is a sinner do such signs?" And there was a division among them.

17They said to the blind man again, "What do you say about Him because He opened your eyes?"

He said, "He is a prophet."

18But the Jews did not believe concerning him, that he had been blind and received his sight, until they called the parents of him who had received his sight. 19And they asked them, saying, "Is this your son, who you say was born blind? How then does he now see?"

20His parents answered them and said, "We know that this is our son, and that he was born blind; 21but by what means he now sees we do not know, or who opened his eyes we do not know. He is of age; ask him. He will speak for himself." 22His parents said these *things* because they feared the Jews, for the Jews had agreed already that if anyone confessed *that* He *was* Christ, he would be put out of the synagogue. 23Therefore his parents said, "He is of age; ask him."

24So they again called the man who was blind, and said to him, "Give God the glory! We know that this Man is a sinner."

25He answered and said, "Whether He is a sinner *or not* I do not know. One thing I know: that though I was blind, now I see."

26Then they said to him again, "What did He do to you? How did He open your eyes?"

27He answered them, "I told you already, and you did not listen. Why do you want to hear *it* again? Do you also want to become His disciples?"

28Then they reviled him and said, "You are His disciple, but we are Moses' disciples. 29We know that God spoke to Moses; *as for* this *fellow*, we do not know where He is from."

30The man answered and said to them, "Why, this is a marvelous thing, that you do not know where He is from; yet He has opened my eyes! 31Now we know that God does not hear sinners; but if anyone is a worshiper of God and does His will, He hears him. 32Since the world began it has been unheard of that anyone opened the eyes of one who was born blind. 33If this Man were not from God, He could do nothing."

34They answered and said to him, "You were completely born in sins, and are you teaching us?" And they cast him out.

TRUE VISION AND TRUE BLINDNESS

35Jesus heard that they had cast him out; and when He had found him, He said to him, "Do you believe in the Son of God?"[a]

36He answered and said, "Who is He, Lord, that I may believe in Him?"

9:35[a] NU-Text reads *Son of Man*.

for doing both. After all, he didn't volunteer for the disease or the deliverance. But he does neither. No, "he worshiped Him" (v. 38). Don't you know he knelt? Don't you think he wept? And how could he keep from wrapping his arms around the waist of the One who gave him sight? He worshiped Him.

And when you see Him, you will too.

APPLICATION

Do Jesus' miracles seem hard to believe? God can defy the laws of time and space because He created them. Miracles are easily within God's power to perform. Remember, you serve a powerful God. Go ahead, then, and tell Him how you need His help today.

FOR YOUR JOURNEY

10:1–42

SITUATION
The parable of the Good Shepherd described Jesus' role perfectly. Unlike a hired worker, Jesus, through love and affection, offered to lay down His life for His flock. Believers trust and know Him.

OBSERVATION
Christ is our faithful shepherd. Put your trust in Him. He wants to give you life to the fullest!

INSPIRATION
Heaven never exports monotony. Christ once

³⁷And Jesus said to him, "You have both seen Him and it is He who is talking with you."

³⁸Then he said, "Lord, I believe!" And he worshiped Him.

³⁹And Jesus said, "For judgment I have come into this world, that those who do not see may see, and that those who see may be made blind."

⁴⁰Then *some* of the Pharisees who were with Him heard these words, and said to Him, "Are we blind also?"

⁴¹Jesus said to them, "If you were blind, you would have no sin; but now you say, 'We see.' Therefore your sin remains."

JESUS THE TRUE SHEPHERD

10 "Most assuredly, I say to you, he who does not enter the sheepfold by the door, but climbs up some other way, the same is a thief and a robber. ²But he who enters by the door is the shepherd of the sheep. ³To him the doorkeeper opens, and the sheep hear his voice; and he calls his own sheep by name and leads them out. ⁴And when he brings out his own sheep, he goes before them; and the sheep follow him, for they know his

---

THE MAN BLIND FROM BIRTH

"Now as Jesus passed by, He saw a man who was blind from birth. And His disciples asked Him, saying, 'Rabbi, who sinned, this man or his parents, that he was born blind?'" (John 9:1–2).

The disciples assume the man's blindness is a punishment. Jesus tells them, no, it's so "the works of God should be revealed in him" (9:3).

Then Jesus "spat on the ground and made clay with the saliva; and He anointed the eyes of the blind man with the clay" (9:6).

One would think such a marvelous, miraculous work of God—a blind man's sight being restored—would unleash a tidal wave of joy throughout the city. One would be wrong. Jesus, you see, performed this healing on the Sabbath (see 9:14).

The response of the religious elite was appalling: "If Jesus made clay, then clearly He engaged in labor! We let Him mix up some spit and dirt today, and by next Sabbath, we'll have people making mortar

and doing home improvements! Besides, this wasn't exactly an *emergency* situation. It's not like the man couldn't breathe. He simply couldn't see. This could have waited a day."

When that's your perspective, when that's your callous takeaway from a bona fide miracle, you have serious vision problems. The Pharisees didn't see the soul in need; they saw a rule violation. Instead of compassion, they doled out contempt. Instead of celebration, they engaged in condemnation. And when the man simply shared what Jesus had done for him, "they cast him out" (9:34).

The story ends well, however. Jesus found the man and introduced Himself as the Son of God (see 9:35). Seeing Jesus for the first time, the man exercised faith and worshiped Him (see 9:38).

voice. ⁵Yet they will by no means follow a stranger, but will flee from him, for they do not know the voice of strangers." ⁶Jesus used this illustration, but they did not understand the things which He spoke to them.

JESUS THE GOOD SHEPHERD

⁷Then Jesus said to them again, "Most assuredly, I say to you, I am the door of the sheep. ⁸All who *ever* came before Me*ᵃ* are thieves and robbers, but the sheep did not hear them. ⁹I am the door. If anyone enters by Me, he will be saved, and will go in and out and find pasture. ¹⁰The thief does not come except to steal, and to kill, and to destroy. I have come that they may have life, and that they may have *it* more abundantly.

¹¹"I am the good shepherd. The good shepherd gives His life for the sheep. ¹²But a hireling, *he who is* not the shepherd, one who does not own the sheep, sees the wolf coming and leaves the sheep and flees; and the wolf catches the sheep and scatters them. ¹³The hireling flees because he is a hireling and does not care about the sheep. ¹⁴I am the good shepherd; and I know My *sheep,* and am known by My own. ¹⁵As the Father knows Me, even so I know the Father; and I lay down My life for the sheep. ¹⁶And other sheep I have which are not of this fold; them also I must bring, and they will hear My voice; and there will be one flock *and* one shepherd.

¹⁷"Therefore My Father loves Me, because I lay down My life that I may take it again. ¹⁸No one takes it from Me, but I lay it down of Myself. I have power to lay it down, and I have power to take it again. This command I have received from My Father."

¹⁹Therefore there was a division again among the Jews because of these sayings. ²⁰And many of them said, "He has a demon and is mad. Why do you listen to Him?"

²¹Others said, "These are not the words of one who has a demon. Can a demon open the eyes of the blind?"

THE SHEPHERD KNOWS HIS SHEEP

²²Now it was the Feast of Dedication in Jerusalem, and it was winter. ²³And Jesus walked in the temple, in Solomon's porch. ²⁴Then the Jews surrounded Him and said to Him, "How long do You keep us in doubt? If You are the Christ, tell us plainly."

²⁵Jesus answered them, "I told you, and you do not believe. The works that I do in My Father's name, they bear witness of Me. ²⁶But you do not believe, because you are not of My sheep, as I said to you.*ᵃ* ²⁷My sheep hear My voice, and I know them, and they follow Me. ²⁸And I give them eternal life, and they shall never perish; neither shall anyone snatch them out of My hand. ²⁹My Father, who has given *them* to Me, is greater than all; and no one is able to snatch *them* out of My Father's hand. ³⁰I and *My* Father are one."

RENEWED EFFORTS TO STONE JESUS

³¹Then the Jews took up stones again to stone Him. ³²Jesus answered them, "Many good works I have shown you from My Father. For which of those works do you stone Me?"

³³The Jews answered Him, saying, "For a good work we do

10:8 *ᵃ* M-Text omits *before Me.*   10:26 *ᵃ* NU-Text omits *as I said to you.*

announced: "I have come that they may have life, and that they may have it more abundantly" (v. 10). Nor does God author loneliness. Among our Maker's first recorded words were these: "It is not good that man should be alone" (Gen. 2:18).

He gets no argument from us. We may relish moments of solitude—but a lifetime of it? No way. Many of us, however, are too fluent in the language of loneliness.

No one knows me, we think. People know my name, but not my heart. They know my face, but not my feelings. I have a Social Security number, but not a soul mate. No one really knows me. And . . .

No one's near me. We hunger for physical contact. Ever since Eve emerged from the bone of Adam, we've been reaching out to touch one another. We need to make a connection. And we need to make a difference.

The anthem of the lonely heart has a third verse: *No one needs me.* The kids used to need me . . . The business once needed me . . . My spouse never needs me . . . Lonely people fight feelings of insignificance.

What do you do with such thoughts? *No one knows me. No one's near me. No one needs me.* How do you cope with such cries for significance?

Some stay busy; others stay drunk. Some buy pets; others buy lovers. Some seek therapy. And a few seek God.

He invites us all to. God's treatment for insignificance won't lead you to a bar or dating service, a spouse or social club. God's ultimate cure for the common life takes you to a manger.

APPLICATION
Are you living life to the fullest? If not, why not? Jesus came to give you a life of joy, peace, and fulfillment.

11:1–57

SITUATION
Jesus traveled from villages beyond the Jordan River to Bethany to raise Lazarus from the dead. Bethany was about two miles east of Jerusalem, and this miracle attracted the attention of many people, including the chief priests and Pharisees. As a result, the people welcomed Him into Jerusalem like a king, but the Pharisees sought to kill Him.

OBSERVATION
Jesus knew Lazarus would die, but He showed His power by raising him from the dead. Before seeing Him perform this great miracle, however, we see that Jesus was sensitive to grief and pain.

INSPIRATION
Have you been there? Have you been called to stand at the thin line that separates the living from the dead? Have you lain awake at night listening to machines pumping air in and out of your lungs? Have you watched sickness corrode and atrophy the body of a friend? Have you lingered behind at the cemetery long after the others have left, gazing in disbelief at the metal casket that contains the body that contained the soul of the one you can't believe is gone?

If so, then this canyon is not unfamiliar to you. Standing on the edge of the canyon draws all of life into perspective. What matters and what doesn't are easily distinguished.

It is possible that I'm addressing someone who is walking the canyon wall. If this is the case, please read the rest of this piece very carefully. Look carefully at the scene described in John 11.

In this scene there are two people: Martha and Jesus. And for all practical purposes they are the only two people in the universe.

not stone You, but for blasphemy, and because You, being a Man, make Yourself God."

34Jesus answered them, "Is it not written in your law, 'I said, "You are gods"'?*a* 35If He called them gods, to whom the word of God came (and the Scripture cannot be broken), 36do you say of Him whom the Father sanctified and sent into the world, 'You are blaspheming,' because I said, 'I am the Son of God'? 37If I do not do the works of My Father, do not believe Me; 38but if I do, though you do not believe Me, believe the works, that you may know and believe*a* that the Father *is* in Me, and I in Him." 39Therefore they sought again to seize Him, but He escaped out of their hand.

THE BELIEVERS BEYOND JORDAN

40And He went away again beyond the Jordan to the place where John was baptizing at first, and there He stayed. 41Then many came to Him and said, "John performed no sign, but all the things that John spoke about this Man were true." 42And many believed in Him there.

THE DEATH OF LAZARUS

11 Now a certain *man* was sick, Lazarus of Bethany, the town of Mary and her sister Martha. 2It was *that* Mary who anointed the Lord with fragrant oil and wiped His feet with her hair, whose brother Lazarus was sick. 3Therefore the sisters sent to Him, saying, "Lord, behold, he whom You love is sick."

4When Jesus heard *that,* He said, "This sickness is not unto death, but for the glory of God, that the Son of God may be glorified through it."

5Now Jesus loved Martha and her sister and Lazarus. 6So, when He heard that he was sick, He stayed two more days in the place where He was. 7Then after this He said to *the* disciples, "Let us go to Judea again."

8*The* disciples said to Him, "Rabbi, lately the Jews sought to stone You, and are You going there again?"

9Jesus answered, "Are there not twelve hours in the day? If anyone walks in the day, he does not stumble, because he sees the light of this world. 10But if one walks in the night, he stumbles, because the light is not in him." 11These things He said, and after that He said to them, "Our friend Lazarus sleeps, but I go that I may wake him up."

12Then His disciples said, "Lord, if he sleeps he will get well." 13However, Jesus spoke of his death, but they thought that He was speaking about taking rest in sleep.

14Then Jesus said to them plainly, "Lazarus is dead. 15And I am glad for your sakes that I was not there, that you may believe. Nevertheless let us go to him."

16Then Thomas, who is called the Twin, said to his fellow disciples, "Let us also go, that we may die with Him."

I AM THE RESURRECTION AND THE LIFE

17So when Jesus came, He found that he had already been in the tomb four days. 18Now Bethany was near Jerusalem, about two miles*a* away. 19And many of the Jews had joined the women

10:34*a* Psalm 82:6   10:38*a* NU-Text reads *understand.*   11:18*a* Literally *fifteen stadia*

around Martha and Mary, to comfort them concerning their brother.

²⁰Then Martha, as soon as she heard that Jesus was coming, went and met Him, but Mary was sitting in the house. ²¹Now Martha said to Jesus, "Lord, if You had been here, my brother would not have died. ²²But even now I know that whatever You ask of God, God will give You."

²³Jesus said to her, "Your brother will rise again."

²⁴Martha said to Him, "I know that he will rise again in the resurrection at the last day."

²⁵Jesus said to her, "I am the resurrection and the life. He who believes in Me, though he may die, he shall live. ²⁶And whoever lives and believes in Me shall never die. Do you believe this?"

²⁷She said to Him, "Yes, Lord, I believe that You are the Christ, the Son of God, who is to come into the world."

JESUS AND DEATH, THE LAST ENEMY

²⁸And when she had said these things, she went her way and secretly called Mary her sister, saying, "The Teacher has come and is calling for you." ²⁹As soon as she heard *that,* she arose quickly and came to Him. ³⁰Now Jesus had not yet come into the town, but was*ᵃ* in the place where Martha met Him. ³¹Then the Jews who were with her in the house, and comforting her, when they saw that Mary rose up quickly and went out, followed her, saying, "She is going to the tomb to weep there."*ᵃ*

³²Then, when Mary came where Jesus was, and saw Him, she fell down at His feet, saying to Him, "Lord, if You had been here, my brother would not have died."

³³Therefore, when Jesus saw her weeping, and the Jews who came with her weeping, He groaned in the spirit and was troubled. ³⁴And He said, "Where have you laid him?"

They said to Him, "Lord, come and see."

³⁵Jesus wept. ³⁶Then the Jews said, "See how He loved him!" ³⁷And some of them said, "Could not this Man, who opened the eyes of the blind, also have kept this man from dying?"

LAZARUS RAISED FROM THE DEAD

³⁸Then Jesus, again groaning in Himself, came to the tomb. It was a cave, and a stone lay against it. ³⁹Jesus said, "Take away the stone."

Martha, the sister of him who was dead, said to Him, "Lord, by this time there is a stench, for he has been *dead* four days."

⁴⁰Jesus said to her, "Did I not say to you that if you would believe you would see the glory of God?" ⁴¹Then they took away the stone *from the place* where the dead man was lying.*ᵃ* And Jesus lifted up *His* eyes and said, "Father, I thank You that You have heard Me. ⁴²And I know that You always hear Me, but because of the people who are standing by I said *this,* that they may believe that You sent Me." ⁴³Now when He had said these things, He cried with a loud voice, "Lazarus, come forth!" ⁴⁴And he who had died came out bound hand and foot with graveclothes, and

---

11:30*ᵃ*NU-Text adds *still.*   11:31*ᵃ*NU-Text reads *supposing that she was going to the tomb to weep there.*   11:41*ᵃ*NU-Text omits *from the place where the dead man was lying.*

Her words were full of despair. "If You had been here . . ." She stares into the Master's face with confused eyes. Lazarus was dead. And the one man who could have made a difference didn't. He hadn't even made it for the burial.

You see, if God is God anywhere, He has to be God in the face of death. Pop psychology can deal with depression. Pep talks can deal with pessimism. Prosperity can handle hunger. But only God can deal with our ultimate dilemma—death. And only the God of the Bible has dared to stand on the canyon's edge and offer an answer.

Jesus then made one of those claims that place Him either on the throne or in the asylum: "Your brother will rise again" (v. 23).

Martha misunderstood. (Who wouldn't have?) "I know that he will rise again in the resurrection at the last day" (v. 24).

That wasn't what Jesus meant. Imagine the setting: Jesus has intruded on the enemy's turf; He's standing in Satan's territory, Death Canyon. His stomach turns as He smells the sulfuric stench of the ex-angel, and He winces as He hears the oppressed wails of those trapped in the prison. Satan has been here. He has violated one of God's creations.

With His foot planted on the serpent's head, Jesus speaks loudly enough that His words echo off the canyon walls.

"I am the resurrection and the life. He who believes in Me, though he may die, he shall live. And whoever lives and believes in Me shall never die. Do you believe this?" (vv. 25–26).

Life confronts death—and wins! The wind stops. A cloud blocks the sun and a bird chirps in the distance while a humiliated snake slithers between the rocks and disappears into the ground.

But Jesus isn't through with Martha. With eyes locked

on hers He asks the greatest question found in Scripture, a question meant as much for you and me as for Martha.

"Do you believe this?"

This is a canyon question. For then we must face ourselves as we really are: rudderless humans tail-spinning toward disaster. And we are forced to see Him for what He claims to be: our only hope.

APPLICATION

Are there ways to imitate Jesus' care and compassion for others in times of deep hurt? Responding to grief with your own emotion offers greater comfort than words.

his face was wrapped with a cloth. Jesus said to them, "Loose him, and let him go."

THE PLOT TO KILL JESUS

⁴⁵Then many of the Jews who had come to Mary, and had seen the things Jesus did, believed in Him. ⁴⁶But some of them went away to the Pharisees and told them the things Jesus did. ⁴⁷Then the chief priests and the Pharisees gathered a council and said, "What shall we do? For this Man works many signs. ⁴⁸If we let Him alone like this, everyone will believe in Him, and the Romans will come and take away both our place and nation."

⁴⁹And one of them, Caiaphas, being high priest that year, said to them, "You know nothing at all, ⁵⁰nor do you consider that it is expedient for us* that one man should die for the people, and not that the whole nation should perish." ⁵¹Now this he did not say on his own *authority;* but being high priest that year he prophesied that Jesus would die for the nation, ⁵²and not for that nation only, but also that He would gather together in one the children of God who were scattered abroad.

⁵³Then, from that day on, they plotted to put Him to death. ⁵⁴Therefore Jesus no longer walked openly among the Jews, but

---

11:50*ᵃ*NU-Text reads *you.*

Jesus Through the Bible

Jesus: The Resurrection and the Life

As youngsters, we neighborhood kids would play street football. The minute we got home from school, we'd drop the books and hit the pavement. The kid across the street had a dad with a great arm and a strong addiction to football. As soon as he'd pull in the driveway from work we'd start yelling for him to come and play ball. He couldn't resist. Out of fairness he'd always ask, "Which team is losing?" Then he would join that team, which often seemed to be mine.

His appearance in the huddle changed the whole ball game. He was confident, strong, and most of all, he had a plan. We'd circle around him, and he'd look at us and say, "Okay boys, here is what we are going to do." The other side was groaning before we left the huddle. You see, we not only had a new plan, we had a new leader.

He brought new life to our team. God does precisely the same. We didn't need a new play; we needed a new plan. We didn't need to trade positions; we needed a new player. That player is Jesus Christ, God's firstborn Son.

"Because of His great love with which He loved us, even when we were dead in trespasses,

made us alive together with Christ (by grace you have been saved)" (Eph. 2:4–5). God's solution is not to preserve the dead—but to raise the dead. "Therefore, if anyone is in Christ, he is a new creation; old things have passed away; behold, all things have become new" (2 Cor. 5:17).

What Jesus did with Lazarus, He is willing to do with us. Which is good to know, for what Martha said about Lazarus can be said about us: "Lord, by this time there is a stench, for he has been dead four days" (John 11:39). Martha was speaking for us all. The human race is dead, and there is a bad smell. We have been dead and buried a long time. We don't need someone to fix us up. We need someone to raise us up. In the muck and mire of what we call life, there is death, and we have been in it so long we've grown accustomed to the stink.

But Christ hasn't. And Christ can't stand the thought of His kids rotting in the cemetery. So He comes in and calls us out. We are the corpse, and He is the corpse-caller. We are the dead, and He is the dead-raiser. Our task is not to get up, but to admit we are dead. The only ones who remain in the grave are the ones who don't think they are there.

For more on Jesus Through the Bible, see Jesus: His Special Clothing.

went from there into the country near the wilderness, to a city called Ephraim, and there remained with His disciples.

⁵⁵And the Passover of the Jews was near, and many went from the country up to Jerusalem before the Passover, to purify themselves. ⁵⁶Then they sought Jesus, and spoke among themselves as they stood in the temple, "What do you think—that He will not come to the feast?" ⁵⁷Now both the chief priests and the Pharisees had given a command, that if anyone knew where He was, he should report *it*, that they might seize Him.

THE ANOINTING AT BETHANY

12 Then, six days before the Passover, Jesus came to Bethany, where Lazarus was who had been dead,ᵃ whom He had raised from the dead. ²There they made Him a supper; and Martha served, but Lazarus was one of those who sat at the table with Him. ³Then Mary took a pound of very costly oil of spikenard, anointed the feet of Jesus, and wiped His feet with her hair. And the house was filled with the fragrance of the oil.

⁴But one of His disciples, Judas Iscariot, Simon's *son,* who would betray Him, said, ⁵"Why was this fragrant oil not sold for three hundred denariiᵃ and given to the poor?" ⁶This he said, not that he cared for the poor, but because he was a thief, and had the money box; and he used to take what was put in it.

⁷But Jesus said, "Let her alone; she has keptᵃ this for the day of My burial. ⁸For the poor you have with you always, but Me you do not have always."

THE PLOT TO KILL LAZARUS

⁹Now a great many of the Jews knew that He was there; and they came, not for Jesus' sake only, but that they might also see Lazarus, whom He had raised from the dead. ¹⁰But the chief priests plotted to put Lazarus to death also, ¹¹because on account of him many of the Jews went away and believed in Jesus.

THE TRIUMPHAL ENTRY

¹²The next day a great multitude that had come to the feast, when they heard that Jesus was coming to Jerusalem, ¹³took branches of palm trees and went out to meet Him, and cried out:

"Hosanna!
'Blessed *is* He who comes in the name of the LORD!'ᵃ
The King of Israel!"

¹⁴Then Jesus, when He had found a young donkey, sat on it; as it is written:

15 "Fear not, daughter of Zion;
Behold, your King is coming,
Sitting on a donkey's colt."ᵃ

¹⁶His disciples did not understand these things at first; but when Jesus was glorified, then they remembered that these

---

12:1ᵃNU-Text omits *who had been dead.*   12:5ᵃAbout one year's wages for a worker   12:7ᵃNU-Text reads *that she may keep.*   12:13ᵃPsalm 118:26   12:15ᵃZechariah 9:9

FOR YOUR JOURNEY

12:1–50

SITUATION

Several groups turned out to see Jesus in the days just prior to His death. Some Jews still believed He was about to set up an earthly political kingdom. Others, especially the Pharisees, opposed Jesus.

OBSERVATION

Jesus proclaimed His kingship with an entry suitable for a king. In Jerusalem, He engaged the leaders and common folks alike in final words of teaching. He explained why He had to die and summarized His overall message. Judas, however, turned against Jesus.

INSPIRATION

God gave Martha a bass drum of service. God gave Mary a flute for praise. And God gave Lazarus a trumpet. And he stood on center stage and played it.

God still gives trumpets. God still calls people from the pits. God still gives pinch-me-I'm-dreaming, too-good-to-be-true testimonies. But not everyone has a dramatic testimony. Who wants a band full of trumpets?

Some convert the lost. Some encourage the saved. And some keep the movement in step. All are needed.

If God has called you to be a Martha, then serve! Remind the rest of us that there is evangelism in feeding the poor and there is worship in nursing the sick.

If God has called you to be a Mary, then worship! Remind the rest of us that we don't have to be busy to be holy. Urge us with your example to put down our clipboards and megaphones and be quiet in worship.

If God has called you to be a Lazarus, then testify. Remind the rest of us that we, too, have a story to tell. We, too, have neighbors who are lost. We, too, have died and been resurrected.

Each of us has our place at the table.

Except one. There was one at Martha's house who didn't find his place. Though he had been near Jesus longer than any of the others, he was furthest in his faith. His name was Judas. He was a thief. When Mary poured the perfume, he feigned spirituality. "The perfume could have been sold and given to the poor," he said. But Jesus knew Judas's heart, and Jesus defended Mary's worship. Years later, John, too, knew Judas's heart, and John explained that Judas was a thief (see v. 6). And all these years he had been dipping his hand in the treasury. The reason he wanted the perfume to be sold and the money put in the treasury was so that he could get his hands on it.

What a sad ending to a beautiful story. But what an appropriate ending. For in every church there are those like Martha who take time to serve. There are those like Mary who take time to worship. There are those like Lazarus who take time to testify.

And there are those like Judas who take, take, take, and never give in return. Are you a Judas? I ask the question carefully, yet honestly. Are you near Christ but far from His heart? Are you at the dinner with a sour soul? Are you always criticizing the gifts of others yet seldom, if ever, giving your own? Are you benefiting from the church while never giving to it? Do others give sacrificially while you give miserly? Are you a Judas?

Do you take, take, take, and never give? If so, you are the Judas in this story.

If you are a Martha, be strengthened. God sees your service.

If you are a Mary, be encouraged. God receives your worship.

If you are a Lazarus, be strong. God honors your conviction.

But if you are a Judas, be warned. God sees your selfishness.

things were written about Him and *that* they had done these things to Him.

17Therefore the people, who were with Him when He called Lazarus out of his tomb and raised him from the dead, bore witness. 18For this reason the people also met Him, because they heard that He had done this sign. 19The Pharisees therefore said among themselves, "You see that you are accomplishing nothing. Look, the world has gone after Him!"

THE FRUITFUL GRAIN OF WHEAT

20Now there were certain Greeks among those who came up to worship at the feast. 21Then they came to Philip, who was from Bethsaida of Galilee, and asked him, saying, "Sir, we wish to see Jesus."

22Philip came and told Andrew, and in turn Andrew and Philip told Jesus.

23But Jesus answered them, saying, "The hour has come that the Son of Man should be glorified. 24Most assuredly, I say to you, unless a grain of wheat falls into the ground and dies, it remains alone; but if it dies, it produces much grain. 25He who loves his life will lose it, and he who hates his life in this world will keep it for eternal life. 26If anyone serves Me, let him follow Me; and where I am, there My servant will be also. If anyone serves Me, him *My* Father will honor.

JESUS PREDICTS HIS DEATH ON THE CROSS

27"Now My soul is troubled, and what shall I say? 'Father, save Me from this hour'? But for this purpose I came to this hour. 28Father, glorify Your name."

Then a voice came from heaven, *saying,* "I have both glorified *it* and will glorify *it* again."

29Therefore the people who stood by and heard *it* said that it had thundered. Others said, "An angel has spoken to Him."

30Jesus answered and said, "This voice did not come because of Me, but for your sake. 31Now is the judgment of this world; now the ruler of this world will be cast out. 32And I, if I am lifted up from the earth, will draw all *peoples* to Myself." 33This He said, signifying by what death He would die.

34The people answered Him, "We have heard from the law that the Christ remains forever; and how *can* You say, 'The Son of Man must be lifted up'? Who is this Son of Man?"

35Then Jesus said to them, "A little while longer the light is with you. Walk while you have the light, lest darkness overtake you; he who walks in darkness does not know where he is going. 36While you have the light, believe in the light, that you may become sons of light." These things Jesus spoke, and departed, and was hidden from them.

WHO HAS BELIEVED OUR REPORT?

37But although He had done so many signs before them, they did not believe in Him, 38that the word of Isaiah the prophet might be fulfilled, which he spoke:

"Lord, who has believed our report?
And to whom has the arm of the LORD been revealed?"*a*

12:38 *a* Isaiah 53:1

³⁹Therefore they could not believe, because Isaiah said again:

⁴⁰ "He has blinded their eyes and hardened their hearts,
    Lest they should see with *their* eyes,
    Lest they should understand with
        their hearts and turn,
    So that I should heal them."ᵃ

⁴¹These things Isaiah said whenᵃ he saw His glory and spoke of Him.

APPLICATION
How would you describe yourself and your service for God's kingdom? Are you more like Martha, Mary, Lazarus—or Judas?

LAZARUS

Most people have heard the story: a man named Lazarus, a close friend of Jesus, died. Four days after the funeral, Jesus marched into the Bethany Cemetery and ceased the deceased condition of Lazarus. Even in a culture with no Facebook, Twitter, or cable news, within hours, *everyone* was buzzing about the dead man walking.

Lazarus didn't have to do a PR blitz on all the morning and late-night talk shows. But the crowds flocked to him. They wanted to see Jesus, of course. But, right after seeing the Miracle Worker, they wanted to see the living, breathing miracle.

Here's the part of the story many people forget. After this incident, the religious establishment decided they'd had enough of Jesus. They began scheming to kill Him (see John 11:53). Then, as they watched Lazarus's celebrity grow, "the chief priests plotted to put Lazarus to death also, because on account of him many of the Jews went away and believed in Jesus" (12:10–11).

If we weren't grieved by their hard-heartedness, we'd have to laugh at their illogical thinking: "Let's put to death the guy who has just proven He's more powerful than death! And, as a bonus, let's kill the man He just called out of the grave!"

This is like threatening Lois Lane with Superman standing at her side.

Do you think Lazarus lost much sleep when he got wind of these rumors? After all, if you've already overcome death and you're a close friend of the One who says, "I am the resurrection and the life" (11:25), what's there to worry about?

We don't know for sure what became of Lazarus. He's not mentioned again in the Gospels, and the Book of Acts says nothing about him. Tradition says he went to Cyprus, where he later became acquainted with Paul and Barnabas. There, the story goes, he served as a leader in the church for about three decades, until he died . . . again. In fact, if you go to the church of Saint Lazarus in Larnaca, Cyprus, you'll see a sarcophagus engraved with these words: "Lazarus, four days dead, friend of Christ."

Even if Lazarus *is* buried there, it's only temporary. One day Jesus will call his old body out of *that* grave too.

13:1–38

SITUATION

Jesus began to teach in the upper room the night before His death. He looked forward to spending this last Passover with His disciples.

OBSERVATION

Jesus washed His disciples' feet, giving us a significant lesson in servanthood.

INSPIRATION

Of all the times we see the bowing knees of Jesus, none is so precious as when He kneels before His disciples and washes their feet.

It was just before the Feast of the Passover. Jesus knew that the time had come for Him to leave this world and go to the Father. Having loved His own who were in the world, He now showed them the full extent of His love (see vv. 1–5).

It has been a long day. Jerusalem is packed with Passover guests, most of whom clamor for a glimpse of the Teacher. The spring sun is warm. The streets are dry. And the disciples are a long way from home. A splash of cool water would be refreshing.

The disciples enter, one by one, and take their places around the table. On the wall hangs a towel, and on the floor sits a pitcher and a basin. Any one of the disciples could volunteer for the job, but not one does.

After a few moments, Jesus stands and removes His outer garment. He wraps a servant's girdle around His waist, takes up the basin, and kneels before one of the disciples. He unlaces a sandal and gently lifts the foot and places it in the basin, covers it with water, and begins to bathe it. One by one, one grimy foot after another, Jesus works His way down the row.

In Jesus' day the washing of feet was a task reserved not just for

WALK IN THE LIGHT

⁴²Nevertheless even among the rulers many believed in Him, but because of the Pharisees they did not confess *Him,* lest they should be put out of the synagogue; ⁴³for they loved the praise of men more than the praise of God.

⁴⁴Then Jesus cried out and said, "He who believes in Me, believes not in Me but in Him who sent Me. ⁴⁵And he who sees Me sees Him who sent Me. ⁴⁶I have come *as* a light into the world, that whoever believes in Me should not abide in darkness. ⁴⁷And if anyone hears My words and does not believe,ᵃ I do not judge him; for I did not come to judge the world but to save the world. ⁴⁸He who rejects Me, and does not receive My words, has that which judges him—the word that I have spoken will judge him in the last day. ⁴⁹For I have not spoken on My own *authority;* but the Father who sent Me gave Me a command, what I should say and what I should speak. ⁵⁰And I know that His command is everlasting life. Therefore, whatever I speak, just as the Father has told Me, so I speak."

JESUS WASHES THE DISCIPLES' FEET

13 Now before the Feast of the Passover, when Jesus knew that His hour had come that He should depart from this world to the Father, having loved His own who were in the world, He loved them to the end.

²And supper being ended,ᵃ the devil having already put it into the heart of Judas Iscariot, Simon's *son,* to betray Him, ³Jesus, knowing that the Father had given all things into His hands, and that He had come from God and was going to God, ⁴rose from supper and laid aside His garments, took a towel and girded Himself. ⁵After that, He poured water into a basin and began to wash the disciples' feet, and to wipe *them* with the towel with which He was girded. ⁶Then He came to Simon Peter. And *Peter* said to Him, "Lord, are You washing my feet?"

⁷Jesus answered and said to him, "What I am doing you do not understand now, but you will know after this."

⁸Peter said to Him, "You shall never wash my feet!"

Jesus answered him, "If I do not wash you, you have no part with Me."

⁹Simon Peter said to Him, "Lord, not my feet only, but also *my* hands and *my* head!"

¹⁰Jesus said to him, "He who is bathed needs only to wash *his* feet, but is completely clean; and you are clean, but not all of you." ¹¹For He knew who would betray Him; therefore He said, "You are not all clean."

¹²So when He had washed their feet, taken His garments, and sat down again, He said to them, "Do you know what I have done to you? ¹³You call Me Teacher and Lord, and you say well, for *so* I am. ¹⁴If I then, *your* Lord and Teacher, have washed your feet, you also ought to wash one another's feet. ¹⁵For I have given you an example, that you should do as I have done to you. ¹⁶Most assuredly, I say to you, a servant is not greater than his master; nor is he who is sent greater than

---

12:47ᵃNU-Text reads *keep them.*   13:2ᵃNU-Text reads *And during supper.*

he who sent him. ¹⁷If you know these things, blessed are you if you do them.

JESUS IDENTIFIES HIS BETRAYER

¹⁸"I do not speak concerning all of you. I know whom I have chosen; but that the Scripture may be fulfilled, 'He who eats bread with Me*ᵃ* has lifted up his heel against Me.'*ᵇ* ¹⁹Now I tell you before it comes, that when it does come to pass, you may believe that I am He. ²⁰Most assuredly, I say to you, he who receives whomever I send receives Me; and he who receives Me receives Him who sent Me."

²¹When Jesus had said these things, He was troubled in spirit, and testified and said, "Most assuredly, I say to you, one of you will betray Me." ²²Then the disciples looked at one another, perplexed about whom He spoke.

²³Now there was leaning on Jesus' bosom one of His disciples, whom Jesus loved. ²⁴Simon Peter therefore motioned to him to ask who it was of whom He spoke.

²⁵Then, leaning back*ᵃ* on Jesus' breast, he said to Him, "Lord, who is it?"

²⁶Jesus answered, "It is he to whom I shall give a piece of bread when I have dipped *it*." And having dipped the bread, He gave *it* to Judas Iscariot, *the son* of Simon. ²⁷Now after the piece of bread, Satan entered him. Then Jesus said to him, "What you do, do quickly." ²⁸But no one at the table knew for what reason He said this to him. ²⁹For some thought, because Judas had the money box, that Jesus had said to him, "Buy *those things* we need for the feast," or that he should give something to the poor.

³⁰Having received the piece of bread, he then went out immediately. And it was night.

THE NEW COMMANDMENT

³¹So, when he had gone out, Jesus said, "Now the Son of Man is glorified, and God is glorified in Him. ³²If God is glorified in Him, God will also glorify Him in Himself, and glorify Him immediately. ³³Little children, I shall be with you a little while longer. You will seek Me; and as I said to the Jews, 'Where I am going, you cannot come,' so now I say to you. ³⁴A new commandment I give to you, that you love one another; as I have loved you, that you also love one another. ³⁵By this all will know that you are My disciples, if you have love for one another."

JESUS PREDICTS PETER'S DENIAL

³⁶Simon Peter said to Him, "Lord, where are You going?"

Jesus answered him, "Where I am going you cannot follow Me now, but you shall follow Me afterward."

³⁷Peter said to Him, "Lord, why can I not follow You now? I will lay down my life for Your sake."

³⁸Jesus answered him, "Will you lay down your life for My sake? Most assuredly, I say to you, the rooster shall not crow till you have denied Me three times.

---

servants but for the lowest of servants. Every circle has its pecking order, and the circle of household workers was no exception. The servant at the bottom of the totem pole was expected to be the one on his knees with the towel and basin.

In this case the one with the towel and basin is the King of the universe. Hands that shaped the stars now wash away filth. Fingers that formed mountains now massage toes. And the One before whom all nations will one day kneel now kneels before His disciples. Hours before His own death, Jesus' concern is singular. He wants His disciples to know how much He loves them. More than removing dirt, Jesus is removing doubt.

Jesus knows what will happen to His hands at the crucifixion. Within twenty-four hours they will be pierced and lifeless. Of all the times we'd expect Him to ask for the disciples' attention, this would be one. But He doesn't.

You can be sure Jesus knows the future of these feet He is washing. These twenty-four feet will not spend the next day following their Master, defending His cause. These feet will dash for cover at the flash of a Roman sword. Only one pair of feet won't abandon Him in the garden. One disciple won't desert Him at Gethsemane— Judas won't even make it that far! He will abandon Jesus that very night at the table.

I looked for a Bible translation that reads, "Jesus washed all the disciples' feet except the feet of Judas," but I couldn't find one. What a passionate moment when Jesus silently lifts the feet of His betrayer and washes them in the basin! Within hours the feet of Judas, cleansed by the kindness of the One he will betray, will stand in Caiaphas's court.

Behold the gift Jesus gives His followers! He knows what these men are about to do. He knows they are about to perform the vilest act of their

---

13:18 *ᵃ*NU-Text reads *My bread.* *ᵇ*Psalm 41:9   13:25 *ᵃ*NU-Text and M-Text add *thus.*

lives. By morning they will bury their heads in shame and look down at their feet in disgust. And when they do, He wants them to remember how His knees knelt before them and He washed their feet. He wants them to realize those feet are still clean. "What I am doing you do not understand now, but you will know after this" (v. 7).

Remarkable. He forgave their sin before they even committed it. He offered mercy before they even sought it.

APPLICATION
Take personal inventory of your life. Are there people you don't want to be around because you feel you're superior to them? Are there people you wouldn't "lower" yourself to help? Study the idea of servanthood. Ask God to put a particular person in your path over the course of the next few weeks.

FOR YOUR JOURNEY

14:1–31
SITUATION
Jesus knew that the disciples were troubled at the thought of His departure. He reassured them by teaching about the Holy Spirit, who would help them.

OBSERVATION
Death did not need to be a terror to the disciples because Jesus was preparing a place for them.

INSPIRATION
What do we do with these worries? Take your anxieties to the cross—literally. Next time you're worried about your health or house or finances or flights, take a mental trip up the hill. Spend a few moments looking again at the pieces of passion.

Run your thumb over the tip of the spear. Balance a spike in the palm of your hand. Read the wooden sign written in your own language. And as you do,

THE WAY, THE TRUTH, AND THE LIFE

14 "Let not your heart be troubled; you believe in God, believe also in Me. ²In My Father's house are many mansions;*a* if *it were* not *so,* I would have told you. I go to prepare a place for you.*b* ³And if I go and prepare a place for you, I will come again and receive you to Myself; that where I am, *there* you may be also. ⁴And where I go you know, and the way you know."

⁵Thomas said to Him, "Lord, we do not know where You are going, and how can we know the way?"

⁶Jesus said to him, "I am the way, the truth, and the life. No one comes to the Father except through Me.

THE FATHER REVEALED

⁷"If you had known Me, you would have known My Father also; and from now on you know Him and have seen Him."

⁸Philip said to Him, "Lord, show us the Father, and it is sufficient for us."

⁹Jesus said to him, "Have I been with you so long, and yet you have not known Me, Philip? He who has seen Me has seen the Father; so how can you say, 'Show us the Father'? ¹⁰Do you not believe that I am in the Father, and the Father in Me? The words that I speak to you I do not speak on My own *authority;* but the Father who dwells in Me does the works. ¹¹Believe Me that I *am* in the Father and the Father in Me, or else believe Me for the sake of the works themselves.

THE ANSWERED PRAYER

¹²"Most assuredly, I say to you, he who believes in Me, the works that I do he will do also; and greater *works* than these he will do, because I go to My Father. ¹³And whatever you ask in My name, that I will do, that the Father may be glorified in the Son. ¹⁴If you ask*a* anything in My name, I will do *it.*

JESUS PROMISES ANOTHER HELPER

¹⁵"If you love Me, keep*a* My commandments. ¹⁶And I will pray the Father, and He will give you another Helper, that He may abide with you forever— ¹⁷the Spirit of truth, whom the world cannot receive, because it neither sees Him nor knows Him; but you know Him, for He dwells with you and will be in you. ¹⁸I will not leave you orphans; I will come to you.

INDWELLING OF THE FATHER AND THE SON

¹⁹"A little while longer and the world will see Me no more, but you will see Me. Because I live, you will live also. ²⁰At that day you will know that I *am* in My Father, and you in Me, and I in you. ²¹He who has My commandments and keeps them, it is he who loves Me. And he who loves Me will be loved by My Father, and I will love him and manifest Myself to him."

²²Judas (not Iscariot) said to Him, "Lord, how is it that You will manifest Yourself to us, and not to the world?"

14:2 *a* Literally *dwellings*   *b* NU-Text adds a word which would cause the text to read either *if it were not so, would I have told you that I go to prepare a place for you?* or *if it were not so I would have told you; for I go to prepare a place for you.*   14:14 *a* NU-Text adds *Me.*   14:15 *a* NU-Text reads *you will keep.*

23Jesus answered and said to him, "If anyone loves Me, he will keep My word; and My Father will love him, and We will come to him and make Our home with him. 24He who does not love Me does not keep My words; and the word which you hear is not Mine but the Father's who sent Me.

THE GIFT OF HIS PEACE

25"These things I have spoken to you while being present with you. 26But the Helper, the Holy Spirit, whom the Father will send in My name, He will teach you all things, and bring to your remembrance all things that I said to you. 27Peace I leave with you, My peace I give to you; not as the world gives do I give to you. Let not your heart be troubled, neither let it be afraid. 28You have heard Me say to you, 'I am going away and coming *back* to you.' If you loved Me, you would rejoice because I said,*a* 'I am going to the Father,' for My Father is greater than I.

29"And now I have told you before it comes, that when it does come to pass, you may believe. 30I will no longer talk much with you, for the ruler of this world is coming, and he has nothing in Me. 31But that the world may know that I love the Father, and as the Father gave Me commandment, so I do. Arise, let us go from here.

THE TRUE VINE

15 "I am the true vine, and My Father is the vinedresser. 2Every branch in Me that does not bear fruit He takes away;*a* and every *branch* that bears fruit He prunes, that it may bear more fruit. 3You are already clean because of the word which I have spoken to you. 4Abide in Me, and I in you. As the branch cannot bear fruit of itself, unless it abides in the vine, neither can you, unless you abide in Me.

5"I am the vine, you *are* the branches. He who abides in Me, and I in him, bears much fruit; for without Me you can do nothing. 6If anyone does not abide in Me, he is cast out as a branch and is withered; and they gather them and throw *them* into the fire, and they are burned. 7If you abide in Me, and My words abide in you, you will*a* ask what you desire, and it shall be done for you. 8By this My Father is glorified, that you bear much fruit; so you will be My disciples.

LOVE AND JOY PERFECTED

9"As the Father loved Me, I also have loved you; abide in My love. 10If you keep My commandments, you will abide in My love, just as I have kept My Father's commandments and abide in His love.

11"These things I have spoken to you, that My joy may remain in you, and *that* your joy may be full. 12This is My commandment, that you love one another as I have loved you. 13Greater love has no one than this, than to lay down one's life for his friends. 14You are My friends if you do whatever I command you. 15No longer do I call you servants, for a servant does not know what his master is doing; but I have called you friends, for all things that I heard from My Father I have made known

---

14:28*a*NU-Text omits *I said.*   15:2*a*Or *lifts up*   15:7*a*NU-Text omits *you will.*

touch the velvet dirt, moist with the blood of God.

Blood He bled for you.

The spear He took for you.

The nails He felt for you.

The sign He left for you.

He did all of this for you. Knowing this, knowing all He did for you there, don't you think He'll look out for you here?

Or as Paul wrote, "He who did not spare His own Son, but delivered Him up for us all, how shall He not with Him also freely give us all things?" (Rom. 8:32).

Do yourself a favor; take your anxious moments to the cross. Leave them there with your bad moments, your mad moments, and your anxious moments. And may I suggest one more? Your final moment.

Barring the return of Christ first, you and I will have one. A final moment. A final breath. A final widening of the eyes and beating of the heart. In a split second you'll leave what you know and enter what you don't.

That's what bothers us. Death is the great unknown. We're always a bit skittish about the unknown.

Sara certainly was. Denalyn and I thought it was a great idea. We would kidnap the girls from school and take them on a weekend trip. We made reservations at a hotel and cleared the trip with their teachers but kept it a secret from our girls. When we showed up at Sara's fourth grade classroom on Friday afternoon, we thought she'd be thrilled. She wasn't. She was afraid. She didn't want to leave!

As we left, I assured her nothing was wrong. We had come to take her to a fun place. Didn't work. By the time we got to the car, she was crying. She was confused. She didn't like the interruption.

Nor do we. God promises to come at an unexpected hour and take us from the gray world we know to a golden world we don't.

But since we don't, we aren't sure we want to go. We even get upset at the thought of His coming.

For that reason, God wants us to do what Sara finally did—trust her father. "Let not your heart be troubled; you believe in God, believe also in Me," He urged. "If I go and prepare a place for you, I will come again and receive you to Myself; that where I am, there you may be also" (John 14:1–3).

By the way, in a short time Sara relaxed and enjoyed the trip. In fact, she didn't want to come back. You won't want to either.

Troubled about your final moments? Leave them at the foot of the cross.

Leave them there with your bad moments, mad moments, and anxious moments.

About this time someone is thinking, *You know, Max, if I leave all those moments at the cross, I won't have any moments left but good ones.*

Well, what do you know? I guess you won't.

APPLICATION
Make a list of everything you're worrying about—health, finances, family, job, and so on. Ask God to help you see all of them in light of eternity. Thank Him that He's looking out for you.

FOR YOUR JOURNEY

15:1–25

SITUATION
The Old Testament referred to Israel as the vine. The Jews in Jesus' day believed that because they belonged to Israel, they were connected to God. But Israel often failed to produce the fruit God looked for. Jesus made a radical statement by claiming to be the Vine.

OBSERVATION
Jesus emphasized that Christians must produce fruit. He expected that of His

to you. 16You did not choose Me, but I chose you and appointed you that you should go and bear fruit, and *that* your fruit should remain, that whatever you ask the Father in My name He may give you. 17These things I command you, that you love one another.

THE WORLD'S HATRED
18"If the world hates you, you know that it hated Me before *it hated* you. 19If you were of the world, the world would love its own. Yet because you are not of the world, but I chose you out of the world, therefore the world hates you. 20Remember the word that I said to you, 'A servant is not greater than his master.' If they persecuted Me, they will also persecute you. If they kept My word, they will keep yours also. 21But all these things they will do to you for My name's sake, because they do not know Him who sent Me. 22If I had not come and spoken to them, they would have no sin, but now they have no excuse for their sin. 23He who hates Me hates My Father also. 24If I had not done among them the works which no one else did, they would have no sin; but now they have seen and also hated both Me and My Father. 25But *this happened* that the word might be fulfilled which is written in their law, 'They hated Me without a cause.'[a]

THE COMING REJECTION
26"But when the Helper comes, whom I shall send to you from the Father, the Spirit of truth who proceeds from the Father, He will testify of Me. 27And you also will bear witness, because you have been with Me from the beginning.

16 "These things I have spoken to you, that you should not be made to stumble. 2They will put you out of the synagogues; yes, the time is coming that whoever kills you will think that he offers God service. 3And these things they will do to you[a] because they have not known the Father nor Me. 4But these things I have told you, that when the[a] time comes, you may remember that I told you of them.

"And these things I did not say to you at the beginning, because I was with you.

THE WORK OF THE HOLY SPIRIT
5"But now I go away to Him who sent Me, and none of you asks Me, 'Where are You going?' 6But because I have said these things to you, sorrow has filled your heart. 7Nevertheless I tell you the truth. It is to your advantage that I go away; for if I do not go away, the Helper will not come to you; but if I depart, I will send Him to you. 8And when He has come, He will convict the world of sin, and of righteousness, and of judgment: 9of sin, because they do not believe in Me; 10of righteousness, because I go to My Father and you see Me no more; 11of judgment, because the ruler of this world is judged.

12"I still have many things to say to you, but you cannot bear *them* now. 13However, when He, the Spirit of truth, has come, He will guide you into all truth; for He will not speak on His

---

15:25 [a] Psalm 69:4   16:3 [a] NU-Text and M-Text omit *to you.*   16:4 [a] NU-Text reads *their.*

own *authority,* but whatever He hears He will speak; and He will tell you things to come. ¹⁴He will glorify Me, for He will take of what is Mine and declare *it* to you. ¹⁵All things that the Father has are Mine. Therefore I said that He will take of Mine and declare *it* to you.ᵃ

SORROW WILL TURN TO JOY

¹⁶"A little while, and you will not see Me; and again a little while, and you will see Me, because I go to the Father."

¹⁷Then *some* of His disciples said among themselves, "What is this that He says to us, 'A little while, and you will not see Me; and again a little while, and you will see Me'; and, 'because I go to the Father'?" ¹⁸They said therefore, "What is this that He says, 'A little while'? We do not know what He is saying."

¹⁹Now Jesus knew that they desired to ask Him, and He said to them, "Are you inquiring among yourselves about what I said, 'A little while, and you will not see Me; and again a little while, and you will see Me'? ²⁰Most assuredly, I say to you that you will weep and lament, but the world will rejoice; and you will be sorrowful, but your sorrow will be turned into joy. ²¹A woman, when she is in labor, has sorrow because her hour has come; but as soon as she has given birth to the child, she no longer remembers the anguish, for joy that a human being has been born into the world. ²²Therefore you now have sorrow; but I will see you again and your heart will rejoice, and your joy no one will take from you.

²³"And in that day you will ask Me nothing. Most assuredly, I say to you, whatever you ask the Father in My name He will give you. ²⁴Until now you have asked nothing in My name. Ask, and you will receive, that your joy may be full.

JESUS CHRIST HAS OVERCOME THE WORLD

²⁵"These things I have spoken to you in figurative language; but the time is coming when I will no longer speak to you in figurative language, but I will tell you plainly about the Father. ²⁶In that day you will ask in My name, and I do not say to you that I shall pray the Father for you; ²⁷for the Father Himself loves you, because you have loved Me, and have believed that I came forth from God. ²⁸I came forth from the Father and have come into the world. Again, I leave the world and go to the Father."

²⁹His disciples said to Him, "See, now You are speaking plainly, and using no figure of speech! ³⁰Now we are sure that You know all things, and have no need that anyone should question You. By this we believe that You came forth from God."

³¹Jesus answered them, "Do you now believe? ³²Indeed the hour is coming, yes, has now come, that you will be scattered, each to his own, and will leave Me alone. And yet I am not alone, because the Father is with Me. ³³These things I have spoken to you, that in Me you may have peace. In the world you willᵃ have tribulation; but be of good cheer, I have overcome the world."

16:15 ᵃNU-Text and M-Text read *He takes of Mine and will declare it to you.*
16:33 ᵃNU-Text and M-Text omit *will.*

followers then and He expects that of His followers now.

INSPIRATION

God loves to find anything that impedes our growth. Jesus portrays Him as the Good Gardener who cuts and trims the vine. "I am the true vine, and My Father is the vinedresser. Every branch in Me that does not bear fruit He takes away; and every branch that bears fruit He prunes, that it may bear more fruit. You are already clean because of the word which I have spoken to you" (15:1–3).

Jesus likely spoke these words while walking from the upper room to the Garden of Gethsemane. Perhaps He saw a vine hanging over a fence or draped along the wall. He lifted up a section of the plant and explained the chain of command in the universe. God is the Gardener. Jesus is the Vine. We are the grapes.

Vines grew abundantly. Carefully pruned, they produced sweet grapes. But left unkept, they crept everywhere and into everything. The gardener trimmed the vines. Why? So they could bear more fruit. God trims us. Why? For the same reason.

"I . . . appointed you that you should go and bear fruit," He explained, "and that your fruit should remain" (15:16).

A good gardener will do what it takes to help a vine bear fruit. What fruit does God want? Love, joy, peace, patience, kindness, goodness, faithfulness, gentleness, and self-control (see Gal. 5:22–23). These are the fruits of the Spirit. And this is what God longs to see in us. And like a careful gardener, He will clip and cut away anything that interferes.

A good track coach looks into the face of the runner and says, "We can break the record, but this is what it will take." And then the coach lists a regimen of practice and discipline.

A good editor reads the manuscript and says, "This work has

potential, but here is what we need to cut." And the writer groans as the red ink flows.

God lifts up a branch of His vine and says, "You can be fruitful, but I'm going to have to clip some diseased leaves." And though the process is painful, we can see on the soil below us the spotted greenery He has clipped. Arrogance. Vain ambitions. Bad relationships. Dangerous opportunities. Revenge.

Does God take this process lightly? I don't think so. Listen to this serious statement. "Every branch that bears fruit He prunes, that it may bear more fruit" (15:2). The verb "prunes" is from the Greek word *airo*. It has at least two meanings; one is to "cut off," and the other is to "pick up" or "lift up." I believe both are implied.

Before God cuts a fruitless branch, He lifts it up. A gardener does this. He repositions the fruitless branch so it can get more sun or more space. Grapes are not like squash or pumpkins. They don't develop while lying on the ground. They grow better hanging free. A good vinedresser will stretch the vine on the arbor to afford it more air and sun.

You've seen gardeners realign a plant, and you've probably seen God realign a life. The family uprooted and transferred to another city—was it so they could learn to trust God? The person so healthy, suddenly sick—was it to remind him to rely on the Gardener? The income stream dried up—was it God's way of lifting you out of the soil of self and drawing you closer to Himself? Leaders with questionable motives and morals are elected. Is it God's way of stirring people to revival?

God is up to something. He is the busy, active Gardener who clears the field and removes the stones. He constructs the trellises and plants the seeds. He inspects the plants and pulls the weeds. And, most of all, He is good. He is the Good Gardener who cares for His vine.

JESUS PRAYS FOR HIMSELF

17 Jesus spoke these words, lifted up His eyes to heaven, and said: "Father, the hour has come. Glorify Your Son, that Your Son also may glorify You, 2as You have given Him authority over all flesh, that He should*a* give eternal life to as many as You have given Him. 3And this is eternal life, that they may know You, the only true God, and Jesus Christ whom You have sent. 4I have glorified You on the earth. I have finished the work which You have given Me to do. 5And now, O Father, glorify Me together with Yourself, with the glory which I had with You before the world was.

JESUS PRAYS FOR HIS DISCIPLES

6"I have manifested Your name to the men whom You have given Me out of the world. They were Yours, You gave them to Me, and they have kept Your word. 7Now they have known that all things which You have given Me are from You. 8For I have given to them the words which You have given Me; and they have received *them,* and have known surely that I came forth from You; and they have believed that You sent Me.

9"I pray for them. I do not pray for the world but for those whom You have given Me, for they are Yours. 10And all Mine are Yours, and Yours are Mine, and I am glorified in them. 11Now I am no longer in the world, but these are in the world, and I come to You. Holy Father, keep through Your name those whom You have given Me,*a* that they may be one as We *are.* 12While I was with them in the world,*a* I kept them in Your name. Those whom You gave Me I have kept;*b* and none of them is lost except the son of perdition, that the Scripture might be fulfilled. 13But now I come to You, and these things I speak in the world, that they may have My joy fulfilled in themselves. 14I have given them Your word; and the world has hated them because they are not of the world, just as I am not of the world. 15I do not pray that You should take them out of the world, but that You should keep them from the evil one. 16They are not of the world, just as I am not of the world. 17Sanctify them by Your truth. Your word is truth. 18As You sent Me into the world, I also have sent them into the world. 19And for their sakes I sanctify Myself, that they also may be sanctified by the truth.

JESUS PRAYS FOR ALL BELIEVERS

20"I do not pray for these alone, but also for those who will*a* believe in Me through their word; 21that they all may be one, as You, Father, *are* in Me, and I in You; that they also may be one in Us, that the world may believe that You sent Me. 22And the glory which You gave Me I have given them, that they may be one just as We are one: 23I in them, and You in Me; that they may be made perfect in one, and that the world may know that You have sent Me, and have loved them as You have loved Me.

24"Father, I desire that they also whom You gave Me may be with Me where I am, that they may behold My glory which

---

17:2 *a*M-Text reads *shall.*   **17:11** *a*NU-Text and M-Text read *keep them through Your name which You have given Me.*   **17:12** *a*NU-Text omits *in the world.* *b*NU-Text reads *in Your name which You gave Me. And I guarded them;* (or *it;*).   **17:20** *a*NU-Text and M-Text omit *will.*

You have given Me; for You loved Me before the foundation of the world. 25O righteous Father! The world has not known You, but I have known You; and these have known that You sent Me. 26And I have declared to them Your name, and will declare *it,* that the love with which You loved Me may be in them, and I in them."

BETRAYAL AND ARREST IN GETHSEMANE

18 When Jesus had spoken these words, He went out with His disciples over the Brook Kidron, where there was a garden, which He and His disciples entered. 2And Judas, who betrayed Him, also knew the place; for Jesus often met there with His disciples. 3Then Judas, having received a detachment *of troops,* and officers from the chief priests and Pharisees, came there with lanterns, torches, and weapons. 4Jesus therefore, knowing all things that would come upon Him, went forward and said to them, "Whom are you seeking?"

5They answered Him, "Jesus of Nazareth."

Jesus said to them, "I am *He.*" And Judas, who betrayed Him, also stood with them. 6Now when He said to them, "I am *He,*" they drew back and fell to the ground.

7Then He asked them again, "Whom are you seeking?" And they said, "Jesus of Nazareth."

8Jesus answered, "I have told you that I am *He.* Therefore, if you seek Me, let these go their way," 9that the saying might be fulfilled which He spoke, "Of those whom You gave Me I have lost none."

10Then Simon Peter, having a sword, drew it and struck the high priest's servant, and cut off his right ear. The servant's name was Malchus.

11So Jesus said to Peter, "Put your sword into the sheath. Shall I not drink the cup which My Father has given Me?"

BEFORE THE HIGH PRIEST

12Then the detachment *of troops* and the captain and the officers of the Jews arrested Jesus and bound Him. 13And they led Him away to Annas first, for he was the father-in-law of Caiaphas who was high priest that year. 14Now it was Caiaphas who advised the Jews that it was expedient that one man should die for the people.

PETER DENIES JESUS

15And Simon Peter followed Jesus, and so *did* another[a] disciple. Now that disciple was known to the high priest, and went with Jesus into the courtyard of the high priest. 16But Peter stood at the door outside. Then the other disciple, who was known to the high priest, went out and spoke to her who kept the door, and brought Peter in. 17Then the servant girl who kept the door said to Peter, "You are not also *one* of this Man's disciples, are you?"

He said, "I am not."

18Now the servants and officers who had made a fire of coals stood there, for it was cold, and they warmed themselves. And Peter stood with them and warmed himself.

18:15 *a* M-Text reads *the other.*

APPLICATION
What fruit do you see in your life? Do you see how God may be pruning you so that you can bear more and better fruit? Grow closer to Jesus. Yield your life to Him, and allow Him to do anything in your life if it will lead to bearing more fruit.

FOR YOUR JOURNEY

15:26—16:33

SITUATION
The disciples, who lived and worked with Jesus, had been His close friends for three years. They were saddened and afraid to hear Him talk of leaving them. Jesus tried to help His friends see the bigger picture— that God had a purpose and a plan. But He also comforted them by promising to be with them through His Spirit.

OBSERVATION
The Holy Spirit was sent to complete several purposes among both believers and non-believers, including pointing out sin and allowing people to understand truth. The Spirit always gives glory to Jesus. That should be our goal, too.

INSPIRATION
The Spirit seals you. The verb *sealed* stirs a variety of images. To protect a letter, you seal the envelope. To keep air out of a jar, you seal its mouth with a rubber-ringed lid. To keep oxygen from the wine, you seal the opening with cork and wax. To seal a deal, you might sign a contract or notarize a signature. Sealing declares ownership and secures contents.

The most famous New Testament "sealing" occurred with the tomb of Jesus. Roman soldiers rolled a rock over the entrance and "made the tomb secure, sealing the stone" (Matt. 27:66). Archaeologists envision two ribbons stretched in front of the entrance, glued together with hardened wax that bore the imprimatur of the Roman government—SPQR (*Senatus Populusque Romanus*)—as if to say, "Stay away! The contents of this tomb belong to Rome." Their seal, of course, proved futile.

The seal of the Spirit, however, proves forceful. When you accepted Christ, God sealed you with the Spirit. "Having believed, you were sealed with the Holy Spirit of promise" (Eph. 1:13). When hell's interlopers come seeking to snatch you from God, the seal turns them away. He bought you, owns you, and protects you. God paid too high a price to leave you

JESUS QUESTIONED BY THE HIGH PRIEST

19The high priest then asked Jesus about His disciples and His doctrine.

20Jesus answered him, "I spoke openly to the world. I always taught in synagogues and in the temple, where the Jews always meet,*a* and in secret I have said nothing. 21Why do you ask Me? Ask those who have heard Me what I said to them. Indeed they know what I said."

22And when He had said these things, one of the officers who stood by struck Jesus with the palm of his hand, saying, "Do You answer the high priest like that?"

23Jesus answered him, "If I have spoken evil, bear witness of the evil; but if well, why do you strike Me?"

24Then Annas sent Him bound to Caiaphas the high priest.

18:20 *a* NU-Text reads *where all the Jews meet.*

MALCHUS

As a longtime servant of Israel's high priest, he had done it all. He'd started with menial tasks—setting up for meetings, laundering the priestly robes. Then, because he had such an eye for detail, he'd graduated to more important functions. He was Caiaphas's personal concierge and unofficial adviser.

On this particular night Caiaphas had sent him with a group of temple police and religious leaders to arrest "that troublemaker" Jesus. "Our sources tell us He likes to pray in the grove on the Mount of Olives," Caiaphas had whispered. "Find Him and bring Him to me. Tonight!"

The servant smiled outwardly even as he groaned inwardly. It had been a long day. He was exhausted. But off he went with this motley search party: the soldiers, eager to do their job and get back to the barracks; the informant Judas, all jumpy and jittery; the scribes and Pharisees, huffing and puffing their way up toward Gethsemane.

Sure enough, Jesus and His little entourage were there. Judas gave the odd signal: a kiss of greeting. When he did, Jesus stepped out of the shadows. "Whom are you seeking?" He asked.

"Jesus of Nazareth," several people replied in unison.

"I am He," Jesus said (John 18:5). Except that He said it with such authority, the whole group of them fell back on the ground.

The men picked themselves up and rushed at Jesus. When they did, "Simon Peter, having a sword, drew it and struck the high priest's servant, and cut off his right ear. The servant's name was Malchus" (18:10).

Peter surely was aiming at more than an ear.

Jesus rebuked Peter for his violent reaction. Then He actually reached out and touched Malchus's bloody stump of an ear and restored it (see Luke 22:51).

Did Malchus become a believer? Some say yes. God only knows. But from that night on, whenever Malchus heard talk about the carpenter who rose from the dead, he could at least tug at his earlobe and know such a thing was possible.

PETER DENIES TWICE MORE

²⁵Now Simon Peter stood and warmed himself. Therefore they said to him, "You are not also *one* of His disciples, are you?"

He denied *it* and said, "I am not!"

²⁶One of the servants of the high priest, a relative *of him* whose ear Peter cut off, said, "Did I not see you in the garden with Him?" ²⁷Peter then denied again; and immediately a rooster crowed.

IN PILATE'S COURT

²⁸Then they led Jesus from Caiaphas to the Praetorium, and it was early morning. But they themselves did not go into the Praetorium, lest they should be defiled, but that they might eat the Passover. ²⁹Pilate then went out to them and said, "What accusation do you bring against this Man?"

³⁰They answered and said to him, "If He were not an evildoer, we would not have delivered Him up to you."

³¹Then Pilate said to them, "You take Him and judge Him according to your law."

Therefore the Jews said to him, "It is not lawful for us to put anyone to death," ³²that the saying of Jesus might be fulfilled which He spoke, signifying by what death He would die.

³³Then Pilate entered the Praetorium again, called Jesus, and said to Him, "Are You the King of the Jews?"

³⁴Jesus answered him, "Are you speaking for yourself about this, or did others tell you this concerning Me?"

³⁵Pilate answered, "Am I a Jew? Your own nation and the chief priests have delivered You to me. What have You done?"

³⁶Jesus answered, "My kingdom is not of this world. If My kingdom were of this world, My servants would fight, so that I should not be delivered to the Jews; but now My kingdom is not from here."

³⁷Pilate therefore said to Him, "Are You a king then?"

Jesus answered, "You say *rightly* that I am a king. For this cause I was born, and for this cause I have come into the world, that I should bear witness to the truth. Everyone who is of the truth hears My voice."

³⁸Pilate said to Him, "What is truth?" And when he had said this, he went out again to the Jews, and said to them, "I find no fault in Him at all.

TAKING THE PLACE OF BARABBAS

³⁹"But you have a custom that I should release someone to you at the Passover. Do you therefore want me to release to you the King of the Jews?"

⁴⁰Then they all cried again, saying, "Not this Man, but Barabbas!" Now Barabbas was a robber.

THE SOLDIERS MOCK JESUS

19 So then Pilate took Jesus and scourged *Him.* ²And the soldiers twisted a crown of thorns and put *it* on His head, and they put on Him a purple robe. ³Then they said,^a "Hail, King of the Jews!" And they struck Him with their hands.

⁴Pilate then went out again, and said to them, "Behold, I am

19:3 ^aNU-Text reads *And they came up to Him and said.*

unguarded. As Paul writes later, "You were sealed for the day of redemption" (Eph. 4:30).

Your Father has no intention of letting you fall. You can't see Him, but He is present. You are "kept by the power of God" (1 Pet. 1:5). He is "able to keep you from stumbling, and to present you faultless before the presence of His glory with exceeding joy" (Jude 24).

Drink deeply from this truth. God is able to keep you from falling! Does He want you living in fear? No! Just the opposite. "For you did not receive the spirit of bondage again to fear, but you received the Spirit of adoption by whom we cry out, 'Abba, Father.' The Spirit Himself bears witness with our spirit that we are children of God" (Rom. 8:15–16).

APPLICATION

Think of an area where you would like to do better or be more effective for God. Then pray that the Spirit will bring glory to God through you. Ask Him to show you how to be more of a servant so that Christ is more readily seen by others.

 FOR YOUR JOURNEY

17:1–26

SITUATION

This is the longest prayer of Jesus recorded in the Bible. It marked the end of Jesus' earthly ministry but looked forward to the ongoing ministry of the immediate and future disciples. Prayer was an important aspect of Jesus' ministry. Whenever a strategic time approached, Jesus spent time in prayer.

OBSERVATION

The world is a battleground. Constant spiritual and physical warfare wages between the forces of God and Satan. Jesus prayed that God would keep His people pure, give them abundant joy, give them peace and unity, and protect them from Satan's power.

INSPIRATION

Immanuel. The name appears in the same Hebrew form as it did two thousand years ago. *Immanu* means "with us." *El* refers to *Elohim*, or God. Not an "above us God" or a "some-where in the neighborhood God." He came as the "with us God." God with us.

Not "God with the rich" or "God with the religious." But God with *us*. All of us. Russians, Germans, Buddhists, Mormons, truck drivers and taxi drivers, librarians. God with *us*.

God *with* us. Don't we love the word *with*? "Will you go *with* me?" we ask. "To the store, to the hospital, through my life?" God says He will. "I am with you always," Jesus said before He ascended to heaven, "even to the end of the age" (Matt. 28:20). Search for restrictions on the promise; you'll find none. You won't find "I'll be with you if you behave . . . when you believe. I'll be with you on Sundays in worship . . . at mass." No, none of that. There's no withholding tax on God's "with" promise. He is *with* us.

God is with us.

Prophets weren't enough. Apostles wouldn't do. Angels won't suffice. God sent more than miracles and messages. He sent himself; He sent His Son. "The Word became flesh and dwelt among us" (John 1:14).

APPLICATION

Do you have special times reserved only for praying? Remember, Jesus regularly went to a quiet place and talked to God. Set up a prayer plan, keep it for a week, and ask God to bless it.

 FOR YOUR JOURNEY

18:1-27

SITUATION

Events surrounding the crucifixion and the resurrection of Jesus form the climax of all four Gospels. The arrest of Jesus has the stamp of divine plan. Jesus suffered to give us eternal life.

bringing Him out to you, that you may know that I find no fault in Him."

PILATE'S DECISION

5Then Jesus came out, wearing the crown of thorns and the purple robe. And *Pilate* said to them, "Behold the Man!"

6Therefore, when the chief priests and officers saw Him, they cried out, saying, "Crucify *Him*, crucify *Him!*"

Pilate said to them, "You take Him and crucify *Him*, for I find no fault in Him."

7The Jews answered him, "We have a law, and according to our*a* law He ought to die, because He made Himself the Son of God."

8Therefore, when Pilate heard that saying, he was the more afraid, 9and went again into the Praetorium, and said to Jesus, "Where are You from?" But Jesus gave him no answer.

10Then Pilate said to Him, "Are You not speaking to me? Do You not know that I have power to crucify You, and power to release You?"

11Jesus answered, "You could have no power at all against Me unless it had been given you from above. Therefore the one who delivered Me to you has the greater sin."

12From then on Pilate sought to release Him, but the Jews cried out, saying, "If you let this Man go, you are not Caesar's friend. Whoever makes himself a king speaks against Caesar."

13When Pilate therefore heard that saying, he brought Jesus out and sat down in the judgment seat in a place that is called *The* Pavement, but in Hebrew, Gabbatha. 14Now it was the Preparation Day of the Passover, and about the sixth hour. And he said to the Jews, "Behold your King!"

15But they cried out, "Away with *Him*, away with *Him!* Crucify Him!"

Pilate said to them, "Shall I crucify your King?"

The chief priests answered, "We have no king but Caesar!"

16Then he delivered Him to them to be crucified. Then they took Jesus and led *Him* away.*a*

THE KING ON A CROSS

17And He, bearing His cross, went out to a place called *the Place* of a Skull, which is called in Hebrew, Golgotha, 18where they crucified Him, and two others with Him, one on either side, and Jesus in the center. 19Now Pilate wrote a title and put *it* on the cross. And the writing was:

JESUS OF NAZARETH, THE KING OF THE JEWS.

20Then many of the Jews read this title, for the place where Jesus was crucified was near the city; and it was written in Hebrew, Greek, *and* Latin.

21Therefore the chief priests of the Jews said to Pilate, "Do not write, 'The King of the Jews,' but, 'He said, "I am the King of the Jews."'"

22Pilate answered, "What I have written, I have written."

23Then the soldiers, when they had crucified Jesus, took His

19:7 *a* NU-Text reads *the law.*   19:16 *a* NU-Text omits *and led Him away.*

garments and made four parts, to each soldier a part, and also the tunic. Now the tunic was without seam, woven from the top in one piece. 24They said therefore among themselves, "Let us not tear it, but cast lots for it, whose it shall be," that the Scripture might be fulfilled which says:

> "They divided My garments among them,
> And for My clothing they cast lots."[a]

Therefore the soldiers did these things.

BEHOLD YOUR MOTHER

25Now there stood by the cross of Jesus His mother, and His mother's sister, Mary the *wife* of Clopas, and Mary Magdalene. 26When Jesus therefore saw His mother, and the disciple whom He loved standing by, He said to His mother, "Woman, behold your son!" 27Then He said to the disciple, "Behold your mother!" And from that hour that disciple took her to his own *home.*

19:24 [a] Psalm 22:18

Jesus Through the Bible

Jesus: His Special Clothing

Scripture says little about the clothes Jesus wore. We know what His cousin John the Baptist wore. We know what the religious leaders wore. But the clothing of Christ is nondescript: neither so humble as to touch hearts nor so glamorous as to turn heads.

One reference to Jesus' garments is noteworthy. "Then the soldiers, when they had crucified Jesus, took His garments and made four parts, to each soldier a part, and also the tunic. Now the tunic was without seam, woven from the top in one piece. They said therefore among themselves, 'Let us not tear it, but cast lots for it, whose it shall be'" (John 19:23–24).

It must have been Jesus' finest possession. Jewish tradition called for a mother to make such a robe and present it to her son as a departure gift when he left home. Had Mary done this for Jesus? We don't know. But we do know the tunic was without seam, woven from top to bottom. Why is this significant?

Scripture often describes our behavior as the clothes we wear. Garments can symbolize character. And like His garment, Jesus' character was seamless. Coordinated. Unified. He was like His robe: uninterrupted perfection.

"Woven from the top." Jesus wasn't led by His own mind; He was led by the mind of His Fa-

ther. Listen to His words: "Most assuredly, I say to you, the Son can do nothing of Himself, but what He sees the Father do; for whatever He does, the Son also does in like manner . . . I can of Myself do nothing. As I hear, I judge" (5:19, 30).

The character of Jesus was a seamless fabric woven from heaven to earth, from God's thoughts to Jesus' actions. From God's tears to Jesus' compassion. From God's Word to Jesus' response. All one piece. All a picture of the character of Jesus.

But when Christ was nailed to the cross, He took off His robe of seamless perfection and assumed a different wardrobe, the wardrobe of indignity.

The indignity of nakedness. Stripped before His own mother and loved ones. Shamed before His family. *The indignity of failure.* For a few pain-filled hours, the religious leaders were the victors, and Christ appeared the loser. Shamed before His accusers. Worst of all, He wore *the indignity of sin.* Christ "bore our sins in His own body on the tree, that we, having died to sins, might live for righteousness" (1 Pet. 2:24).

The clothing of Christ on the cross? Sin—yours and mine. The sins of all humanity.

For more on Jesus Through the Bible, see Jesus: The Power of God.

with the loop, and let the squirrel run around it into the hole." "Shape a rabbit ear, and then wrap it with a ribbon." Dad said, "Go fast." Your uncle said to take your time. Can't anyone agree? Only on one thing. You need to know how.

Learning to tie your shoes is a rite of passage. Right in there with first grade and first bike is first shoe tying. But, oh, how dreadful is the process.

Just when you think you've made the loops and circled the tree,

IT IS FINISHED

28After this, Jesus, knowing*a* that all things were now accomplished, that the Scripture might be fulfilled, said, "I thirst!" 29Now a vessel full of sour wine was sitting there; and they filled a sponge with sour wine, put *it* on hyssop, and put *it* to His mouth. 30So when Jesus had received the sour wine, He said, "It is finished!" And bowing His head, He gave up His spirit.

JESUS' SIDE IS PIERCED

31Therefore, because it was the Preparation *Day,* that the bodies should not remain on the cross on the Sabbath (for that Sabbath was a high day), the Jews asked Pilate that their legs

---

19:28 *a* M-Text reads *seeing.*

MARY, MOTHER OF JESUS

Everyone had insisted she get some sleep. But in the wee hours of Saturday, Mary decided it was useless. There would be no rest this Sabbath.

After dressing quietly, she tiptoed through the house filled with snores and slipped out the door. Sitting on a bench in the courtyard, she gazed upward at the stars. Memories, like moonlight, began to wash over her.

She recalled another starry night. The angel—how massive he had been! And how frightened she was! Then the strange peace that filled her when she heard herself saying, "Behold the maidservant of the Lord! Let it be to me according to your word" (Luke 1:38).

Tonight's bright star in the east—the morning star, Mary assumed—brought to mind the long-ago Bethlehem trip. The contractions rumbling within her like earthquakes. The frantic, funny way Joseph had scrambled about, creating a delivery room. Closing her eyes, she could still hear her baby's first cries, still see the astonished faces of the shepherds.

She thought about the dedication at the temple eight days later, all those years ago. The sweet old widow named Anna.

The shaky old man who joyfully took the baby out of her arms. The way he oohed and aahed over the child before suddenly frowning, handing Him back, and prophesying the sword that would one day pierce her soul. Obviously he meant today. *Oh, Lord, will I ever get those images out of my mind?*

For several seconds, Mary dabbed at her damp, swollen eyes. Then she told herself, *Think on the good moments.* And there were plenty of those. The way He'd always taken care of her. The gorgeous dinner table He'd made for her fortieth birthday. The time He'd saved her friends in Cana from a total wedding disaster. The first time she heard Him preach. The countless times total strangers came up and told her how He'd changed their lives forever.

As the sky began to lighten, Mary remembered Him saying, "I am the light of the world" (John 8:12).

She stood and smiled. He's definitely the light of mine.

might be broken, and *that* they might be taken away. ³²Then the soldiers came and broke the legs of the first and of the other who was crucified with Him. ³³But when they came to Jesus and saw that He was already dead, they did not break His legs. ³⁴But one of the soldiers pierced His side with a spear, and immediately blood and water came out. ³⁵And he who has seen has testified, and his testimony is true; and he knows that he is telling the truth, so that you may believe. ³⁶For these things were done that the Scripture should be fulfilled, "Not *one* of His bones shall be broken."ᵃ ³⁷And again another Scripture says, "They shall look on Him whom they pierced."ᵃ

JESUS BURIED IN JOSEPH'S TOMB

³⁸After this, Joseph of Arimathea, being a disciple of Jesus, but secretly, for fear of the Jews, asked Pilate that he might take away the body of Jesus; and Pilate gave *him* permission. So he came and took the body of Jesus. ³⁹And Nicodemus, who at first came to Jesus by night, also came, bringing a mixture of myrrh and aloes, about a hundred pounds. ⁴⁰Then they took the body of Jesus, and bound it in strips of linen with the spices, as the custom of the Jews is to bury. ⁴¹Now in the place where He was crucified there was a garden, and in the garden a new tomb in which no one had yet been laid. ⁴²So there they laid Jesus, because of the Jews' Preparation *Day*, for the tomb was nearby.

THE EMPTY TOMB

20 Now the first *day* of the week Mary Magdalene went to the tomb early, while it was still dark, and saw *that* the stone had been taken away from the tomb. ²Then she ran and came to Simon Peter, and to the other disciple, whom Jesus loved, and said to them, "They have taken away the Lord out of the tomb, and we do not know where they have laid Him."

³Peter therefore went out, and the other disciple, and were going to the tomb. ⁴So they both ran together, and the other disciple outran Peter and came to the tomb first. ⁵And he, stooping down and looking in, saw the linen cloths lying *there;* yet he did not go in. ⁶Then Simon Peter came, following him, and went into the tomb; and he saw the linen cloths lying *there,* ⁷and the handkerchief that had been around His head, not lying with the linen cloths, but folded together in a place by itself. ⁸Then the other disciple, who came to the tomb first, went in also; and he saw and believed. ⁹For as yet they did not know the Scripture, that He must rise again from the dead. ¹⁰Then the disciples went away again to their own homes.

MARY MAGDALENE SEES THE RISEN LORD

¹¹But Mary stood outside by the tomb weeping, and as she wept she stooped down *and looked* into the tomb. ¹²And she saw two angels in white sitting, one at the head and the other at the feet, where the body of Jesus had lain. ¹³Then they said to her, "Woman, why are you weeping?"

She said to them, "Because they have taken away my Lord, and I do not know where they have laid Him."

¹⁴Now when she had said this, she turned around and saw

19:36 ᵃ Exodus 12:46; Numbers 9:12; Psalm 34:20　　19:37 ᵃ Zechariah 12:10

you get the rabbit ears in either hand and give them a triumphant yank and, voilà!—a knot. Unbeknownst to you, you've just been inducted into reality.

My friend Roy used to sit on a park bench for a few minutes each morning. He liked to watch the kids gather and play at the bus stop. One day he noticed a little fellow, maybe five or six years of age, struggling to board the bus. While others were climbing on, he was leaning down, frantically trying to disentangle a knotted shoestring. He grew more anxious by the moment, frantic eyes darting back and forth between the shoe and the ride.

All of a sudden it was too late. The door closed.

The boy fell back on his haunches and sighed. That's when he saw Roy. With tear-filled eyes he looked at the man on the bench and asked, "Do you untie knots?"

Jesus loves that request.

Life gets tangled. People mess up. You never outgrow the urge to look up and say, "Help!"

Jesus had a way of appearing at such moments. Peter's empty boat. Nicodemus's empty heart. Matthew has a friend issue. A woman has a health issue. Look who shows up.

Jesus, our next-door Savior.

"Do you untie knots?"

"Yes."

APPLICATION

Remember, God joins our suffering—strengthening and lifting us up so that we can share in His glory.

 FOR YOUR JOURNEY

18:28—19:42

SITUATION

Jewish leaders hoped to crucify Jesus but did not have the authority to do this, so they brought Him to the Roman governor, Pilate. Shrewd Pilate knew that the Jewish leaders wanted him to act as their executioner. He pronounced Jesus innocent and tried to save Him, but finally consented to the crucifixion because of public pressure.

OBSERVATION

Jesus knew that His trial was according to God's will and faced it with humility and self-control. In His cry, "It is finished," we hear the triumphant recognition that He has now fully accomplished God's will and paid for our sins in full.

Jesus standing *there,* and did not know that it was Jesus. ¹⁵Jesus said to her, "Woman, why are you weeping? Whom are you seeking?"

She, supposing Him to be the gardener, said to Him, "Sir, if You have carried Him away, tell me where You have laid Him, and I will take Him away."

¹⁶Jesus said to her, "Mary!"

She turned and said to Him,ᵃ "Rabboni!" (which is to say, Teacher).

¹⁷Jesus said to her, "Do not cling to Me, for I have not yet ascended to My Father; but go to My brethren and say to them, 'I am ascending to My Father and your Father, and *to* My God and your God.'"

20:16 ᵃ NU-Text adds *in Hebrew.*

MARY MAGDALENE

Some are convinced that Mary Magdalene was a prostitute before encountering Christ. Is there any truth to the charge? Or is this claim simply fallacious?

Here's what we know: Magdala was a town in Galilee. Thus Magdalene is an indicator of where Mary was from, not her last name.

Luke tells us Mary was one of a large number of female followers of Jesus who provided financial support to His ministry. Some of these women "had been healed of evil spirits and infirmities," and Mary was a woman "out of whom had come seven demons" (Luke 8:2). This is the one and only explicit detail given in the New Testament about Mary's life prior to meeting Jesus.

The clear implication is that Jesus is the One who set Mary Magdalene free from a life of demonic possession. Based on other Gospel accounts of evil spirits tormenting people, we don't have to know gory details to know Mary's former life was awful. Might that experience have included prostitution? Some think so. Since the sixth century, some have speculated that Mary is the unnamed "sinful" woman who anointed Jesus' feet in Luke 7:36–39. Others have theorized that she is the woman Jesus rescued from stoning in John 8:1–11. Since

neither passage names Mary overtly, we can't say for sure.

What we do know is this:

- She was there at Jesus' death (see Mark 15:40; John 19:25). While many of His disciples hid and other followers watched Him from a distance, Mary was right at the foot of the cross.

- She was there at His burial (see Mark 15:47). While everyone else trickled away, Mary Magdalene followed Joseph and Nicodemus to the garden tomb.

- She was there at His resurrection (see John 20:11–18). Mary Magdalene was the first person to see the risen Christ.

Because of her fierce devotion to Jesus, it seems that only Mary Magdalene witnessed all three of these gospel truths: "Christ died . . . He was buried . . . He rose again" (1 Cor. 15:3–4).

No wonder she received the distinct honor of getting to be the first to share that good news (see John 20:18).

¹⁸Mary Magdalene came and told the disciples that she had seen the Lord,ᵃ and *that* He had spoken these things to her.

THE APOSTLES COMMISSIONED

¹⁹Then, the same day at evening, being the first *day* of the week, when the doors were shut where the disciples were assembled,ᵃ for fear of the Jews, Jesus came and stood in the midst, and said to them, "Peace *be* with you." ²⁰When He had said this, He showed them *His* hands and His side. Then the disciples were glad when they saw the Lord.

²¹So Jesus said to them again, "Peace to you! As the Father has sent Me, I also send you." ²²And when He had said this, He breathed on *them,* and said to them, "Receive the Holy Spirit. ²³If you forgive the sins of any, they are forgiven them; if you retain the *sins* of any, they are retained."

SEEING AND BELIEVING

²⁴Now Thomas, called the Twin, one of the twelve, was not with them when Jesus came. ²⁵The other disciples therefore said to him, "We have seen the Lord."

So he said to them, "Unless I see in His hands the print of the nails, and put my finger into the print of the nails, and put my hand into His side, I will not believe."

²⁶And after eight days His disciples were again inside, and Thomas with them. Jesus came, the doors being shut, and stood in the midst, and said, "Peace to you!" ²⁷Then He said to Thomas, "Reach your finger here, and look at My hands; and reach your hand *here,* and put *it* into My side. Do not be unbelieving, but believing."

²⁸And Thomas answered and said to Him, "My Lord and my God!"

²⁹Jesus said to him, "Thomas,ᵃ because you have seen Me, you have believed. Blessed *are* those who have not seen and *yet* have believed."

THAT YOU MAY BELIEVE

³⁰And truly Jesus did many other signs in the presence of His disciples, which are not written in this book; ³¹but these are written that you may believe that Jesus is the Christ, the Son of God, and that believing you may have life in His name.

BREAKFAST BY THE SEA

21 After these things Jesus showed Himself again to the disciples at the Sea of Tiberias, and in this way He showed *Himself:* ²Simon Peter, Thomas called the Twin, Nathanael of Cana in Galilee, the *sons* of Zebedee, and two others of His disciples were together. ³Simon Peter said to them, "I am going fishing."

They said to him, "We are going with you also." They went out and immediatelyᵃ got into the boat, and that night they caught nothing. ⁴But when the morning had now come, Jesus stood on the shore; yet the disciples did not know that it was Jesus. ⁵Then Jesus said to them, "Children, have you any food?"

20:18ᵃNU-Text reads *disciples, "I have seen the Lord,"....* 20:19ᵃNU-Text omits *assembled.* 20:29ᵃNU-Text and M-Text omit *Thomas.* 21:3ᵃNU-Text omits *immediately.*

INSPIRATION

Pilate wants to let Jesus go. *Just give me a reason,* he thinks, almost aloud. *I'll set you free.*

His thoughts are interrupted by a tap on the shoulder. A messenger leans and whispers. Strange. Pilate's wife has sent word not to get involved in the case. Something about a dream she had.

Pilate walks back to his chair, sits, and stares at Jesus. "Even the gods are on your side?" he states with no explanation.

How many wide eyes have stared at him, pleading for mercy, begging for acquittal?

But the eyes of this Nazarene are calm, silent.

He's not angry with me. He's not afraid. He seems to understand.

"What should I do with Jesus, the one called the Christ?"

What do you do with a man who claims to be God, yet hates religion? What do you do with a man who knows the place and time of His death, yet goes there anyway?

You can reject Him.

Or you can accept Him. You can journey with Him. You can listen for His voice amidst the hundreds of voices and follow Him.

APPLICATION

What resources do you call upon to make tough decisions? Where do you go for advice? How do you process the options? Next time you need to make a decision, pray first. Then pray again all along the way until you decide.

FOR YOUR JOURNEY

20:1–31

SITUATION

The Jewish religious leaders hoped that Pilate, the Roman Governor, would execute Jesus for them. Pilate declared Jesus innocent and tried to facilitate His freedom, but the religious

leaders and Jewish people wouldn't be satisfied until Jesus was killed. Pilate gave in to their demands, and Jesus was publicly crucified.

OBSERVATION

When we're in the midst of the battle, we can remain confident that it's not over until God says, "It is finished!" (John 19:30).

They answered Him, "No."

⁶And He said to them, "Cast the net on the right side of the boat, and you will find *some*." So they cast, and now they were not able to draw it in because of the multitude of fish. ⁷Therefore that disciple whom Jesus loved said to Peter, "It is the Lord!" Now when Simon Peter heard that it was the Lord, he put on *his* outer garment (for he had removed it), and plunged into the sea. ⁸But the other disciples came in the little boat (for they were not far from land, but about two hundred cubits), dragging the net with fish. ⁹Then, as soon as they had come

THOMAS

The patriarch of the Judeo-Christian faith had trouble at times telling the truth, yet nobody calls him Lying Abraham. Israel's great lawgiver once beat a man to death, but he isn't remembered as Murdering Moses. The message of the Bible is that we're not defined by our worst moments. The gospel says that, in Christ, God expunges our failures. Grace, not sin, gets the last word. Aren't you thankful for such good news?

Why then do we persist in speaking of Doubting Thomas?

Thomas was one of Jesus' most loyal followers. The Gospels portray him as reflective, not talkative. On the three occasions where his words are recorded, it's clear Thomas thought long and hard before speaking.

Once, in the wake of a friend's death, Thomas broke the silence, saying that *he* was willing to die for Jesus if it came to that (see John 11:16). On the night before the crucifixion, when Jesus talked cryptically about going away, Thomas let it be known he wasn't keen on the idea of being separated from Jesus (see 14:5).

So when everything came crashing down the following day, Thomas was devastated. They all were, of course, but Thomas seemed to take it especially hard. While the rest huddled together in fear, Thomas went off the grid. He turned off his cell phone.

He didn't check email. On Resurrection Sunday, when Jesus appeared to His disciples, Thomas was nowhere to be found.

He emerged from hiding to find his buddies beside themselves with joy. "We have seen the Lord," they exclaimed. Thomas wasn't buying it: "Unless I see in His hands the print of the nails, and put my finger into the print of the nails, and put my hand into His side, I will not believe" (20:25).

This may sound like hard-heartedness, but it wasn't. We know this because a few days later, when Jesus graciously appeared to Thomas, he fell to his knees and confessed, "My Lord and my God!" (20:28).

Stubborn unbelief says, "I'm happy where I am, and no amount of evidence will change my mind." Honest doubt says, "I want to believe but I'm struggling. I just need a little help."

Doubting Thomas? One week of weakness doesn't tell the whole story of his—or anyone else's—life. Tradition claims Thomas sailed to India to preach the gospel, eventually dying for the risen One who'd resurrected his flagging faith. Sounds more like Trusting Thomas.

to land, they saw a fire of coals there, and fish laid on it, and bread. ¹⁰Jesus said to them, "Bring some of the fish which you have just caught."

¹¹Simon Peter went up and dragged the net to land, full of large fish, one hundred and fifty-three; and although there were so many, the net was not broken. ¹²Jesus said to them, "Come *and* eat breakfast." Yet none of the disciples dared ask Him, "Who are You?"—knowing that it was the Lord. ¹³Jesus then came and took the bread and gave it to them, and likewise the fish.

¹⁴This *is* now the third time Jesus showed Himself to His disciples after He was raised from the dead.

JESUS RESTORES PETER

¹⁵So when they had eaten breakfast, Jesus said to Simon Peter, "Simon, *son* of Jonah,ᵃ do you love Me more than these?"

He said to Him, "Yes, Lord; You know that I love You."

He said to him, "Feed My lambs."

¹⁶He said to him again a second time, "Simon, *son* of Jonah,ᵃ do you love Me?"

He said to Him, "Yes, Lord; You know that I love You."

He said to him, "Tend My sheep."

¹⁷He said to him the third time, "Simon, *son* of Jonah,ᵃ do you love Me?" Peter was grieved because He said to him the third time, "Do you love Me?"

21:15ᵃNU-Text reads *John.*   21:16ᵃNU-Text reads *John.*   21:17ᵃNU-Text reads *John.*

Jesus Through the Bible

Jesus: The Power of God

For three days Jesus' body decayed. It did not rest, mind you. It decayed. The cheeks sank and the skin paled. But after three days the process was reversed. There was a stirring, a stirring deep within the grave . . . and the living Christ stepped forth.

And the moment He stepped forth, everything changed. The resurrection is an exploding flare announcing to all sincere seekers that it is safe to believe. Safe to believe in ultimate justice. Safe to believe in eternal bodies. Safe to believe in heaven as our estate and the earth as its porch. Safe to believe in a time when questions won't keep us awake and pain won't keep us down. Safe to believe in open graves and endless days and genuine praise.

Because we can accept the resurrection story, it is safe to accept the rest of the story.

Because of the resurrection, everything changes. Death changes. It used to be the end; now it is the beginning. The cemetery changes.

People once went there to say goodbye; now they go to say, "We'll be together again." Even the coffin changes. The casket is no longer a box where we hide bodies, but rather a cocoon in which the body is kept until God sets it free to fly.

And someday, according to Christ, He will set us free. He will come back: "I will come again and receive you to Myself" (John 14:3). And to prove that He was serious about His promise, the stone was rolled and His body was raised.

For He knows that someday this world will shake again. In the blink of an eye, as fast as the lightning flashes from the east to the west, He will come back. And everyone will see Him— you will, I will. Bodies will push back the dirt and break the surface of the sea. The earth will tremble, the sky will roar, and those who do not know Him will shudder. But in that hour you will not fear, because you know Him.

but with assurance of complete victory.

March like a Promised Land conqueror. Blast your ram's horn. Sing songs of redemption and declare scriptures of triumph. Marinate your mind with the declaration of Jesus, "It is finished!" (19:30), and the announcement of the angels, "He is not here; for He is risen" (Matt. 28:6). Personalize the

And he said to Him, "Lord, You know all things; You know that I love You."

Jesus said to him, "Feed My sheep. ¹⁸Most assuredly, I say to you, when you were younger, you girded yourself and walked where you wished; but when you are old, you will stretch out your hands, and another will gird you and carry *you* where you do not wish." ¹⁹This He spoke, signifying by what death he would glorify God. And when He had spoken this, He said to him, "Follow Me."

THE BELOVED DISCIPLE AND HIS BOOK

²⁰Then Peter, turning around, saw the disciple whom Jesus loved following, who also had leaned on His breast at the supper,

CONSIDER: *SECOND CHANCES*

The most difficult journey is back to the place where you failed.

Peter is in the boat, on the lake. Once again he's fished all night. Once again the sea has surrendered nothing.

His thoughts are interrupted by a shout from the shore. "Catch any fish?" Peter and John look up. Probably a villager. "No!" they yell. "Try the other side!" the voice shouts. So out sails the net. Peter wraps the rope around his wrist to wait.

But there is no wait. The rope pulls taut and the net catches. Peter begins to bring in the net; reaching down, pulling up, reaching down, pulling up. He's so intense with the task, he misses the message.

John doesn't. "It's the Lord, Peter. It's the Lord!"

Peter plunges into the water, swims to the shore, and stumbles out wet and shivering and stands in front of the friend he betrayed. Jesus has prepared a bed of coals. Both are aware of the last time Peter had stood near a fire. Peter had failed God, but God had come to him.

For one of the few times in his life, Peter is silent. What words would suffice? The moment is too holy for words. God is offering breakfast to the friend who betrayed Him. And Peter is once again finding grace at Galilee.

Now, it's just you and God. You and God both know what you did. And neither one of you is proud of it. What do you do?

You might consider doing what Peter did. Stand in God's presence. Stand in His sight. Stand still and wait. Sometimes that's all a soul can do. Too repentant to speak, but too hopeful to leave—we just stand.

Stand amazed.

He has come back.

He invites you to try again. This time, with Him.

STUDY GUIDE
READ JOHN 21:1-11.

• Why do you think there is such a stigma on admitting failure when we know that even the most successful people fail along the way?

• How do you imagine Peter felt when he saw Jesus for the first time after denying Him?

• Describe a time when you, like Peter, were too preoccupied or busy to recognize God's presence with you.

• Why do you think Peter was in a hurry to see Jesus after his failure?

• What keeps us from running to Jesus after we have failed?

• What personal fears do you think caused Peter earlier to deny Jesus?

• What kinds of fears motivate us to compromise our convictions?

• How do you imagine this experience impacted Peter for the rest of his life?

• What failure in life do you need to revisit with a greater awareness of God's presence?

and said, "Lord, who is the one who betrays You?" [21]Peter, seeing him, said to Jesus, "But Lord, what *about* this man?"

[22]Jesus said to him, "If I will that he remain till I come, what *is that* to you? You follow Me."

[23]Then this saying went out among the brethren that this disciple would not die. Yet Jesus did not say to him that he would not die, but, "If I will that he remain till I come, what *is that* to you?"

[24]This is the disciple who testifies of these things, and wrote these things; and we know that his testimony is true.

[25]And there are also many other things that Jesus did, which if they were written one by one, I suppose that even the world itself could not contain the books that would be written. Amen.

proclamations of Paul: "We are more than conquerors through [Christ]" (Rom. 8:37), and "I can do all things through Christ" (Phil. 4:13). As you do, the demons will begin to scatter. They have no choice but to leave.

APPLICATION

When it looks like you're losing the battle, speak God's words over your circumstances. Loudly declare Romans 8:37 and Philippians 4:13. Enlist some fellow believers to help you proclaim your victory.

 FOR YOUR JOURNEY

21:1–25

SITUATION

John explained that the story has not ended. Jesus Christ formed, commissioned, and empowered His church. The church continued Jesus' ministry.

OBSERVATION

Jesus does not let His followers wallow in failure. He forgave Peter, and He forgives us.

INSPIRATION

Tether your heart to this promise and tighten the knot. Remember the words of John's epistle: "If our heart condemns us, God is greater than our heart, and knows all things" (1 John 3:20). When you feel unforgiven, evict the feelings. Emotions don't get a vote. Go back to Scripture. God's Word holds rank over self-criticism and self-doubt.

As Paul told Titus, "For the grace of God that brings salvation has appeared to all men . . . Speak these things, exhort, and rebuke with all authority. Let no one despise you" (Titus 2:11, 15). Do you know God's grace? Then you can love boldly, live robustly. You can swing from trapeze to trapeze; His safety net will break your fall.

Nothing fosters courage like a clear grasp of grace.

And nothing fosters fear like an ignorance of mercy. May I speak candidly? If you haven't accepted God's forgiveness, you are doomed to fear. Nothing can deliver you from the gnawing realization that you have disregarded your Maker and

disobeyed His instruction. No pill, pep talk, psychiatrist, or possession can set the sinner's heart at ease. You may deaden the fear, but you can't remove it. Only God's grace can.

Have you accepted the forgiveness of Christ? If not, do so. "If we confess our sins, He is faithful and just to forgive us our sins and to cleanse us from all unrighteousness" (1 John 1:9). Your prayer can be as simple as this: *Dear Father, I need forgiveness. I admit that I have turned away from You. Please forgive me. I place my soul in Your hands and my trust in Your grace. Through Jesus I pray, amen.*

Having received God's forgiveness, live forgiven! Jesus has healed your legs, so walk. Jesus has opened the cage of the kennel, so step out. When Jesus sets you free, you are free indeed.

APPLICATION

Name the biggest blunders of your life—have you faced them, admitted them, wondered about them? Because Jesus restores and heals, you can be forgiven.

ACKNOWLEDGMENTS

MAX LUCADO BOOKS
The articles and notes found throughout this edition have been taken from the many years of Max Lucado's teachings, sermons, books, and articles. However, the majority of the features found here were adapted from the following Max Lucado books:

3:16, The Numbers of Hope, copyright © 2007, Thomas Nelson Publishers, Nashville, Tennessee. All rights reserved.

And the Angels Were Silent, copyright © 1992, Questar Publishers, Multnomah Books.

The Applause of Heaven, copyright © 1990, Word, Inc., Dallas, Texas.

Come Thirsty, copyright © 2004, Thomas Nelson Publishers, Nashville, Tennessee. All rights reserved.

Cure for the Common Life, copyright © 2005, W Publishing Group, Nashville, Tennessee. All rights reserved.

Fearless, copyright © 2009, Thomas Nelson Publishers, Nashville, Tennessee. All rights reserved.

Glory Days, copyright © 2015, Thomas Nelson Publishers, Nashville, Tennessee. All rights reserved.

He Chose the Nails, copyright © 2000, W Publishing Group, Nashville, Tennessee. All rights reserved.

He Still Moves Stones, copyright © 1993, Word, Inc., Dallas, Texas.

In the Eye of the Storm, copyright © 1991, Word, Inc., Dallas, Texas.

In the Grip of Grace, copyright © 1993, Word, Inc., Dallas, Texas.

Next Door Savior, copyright © 2003, Thomas Nelson Publishers, Nashville, Tennessee. All rights reserved.

Six Hours One Friday, copyright © 1989, Questar Publishers, Multnomah Books.

When Christ Comes, copyright © 1999, W Publishing Group, Nashville, Tennessee. All rights reserved.

When God Whispers Your Name, copyright © 1994, Word, Inc., Dallas, Texas.

"CONSIDER" STUDIES ADAPTED FROM:
"God's presence" from *In the Eye of the Storm*
"Second Chances" from *He Still Moves Stones*
"Usefulness" from *The Applause of Heaven*
"Where Is God?" from *He Still Moves Stones*

JESUS THROUGH THE BIBLE ARTICLES ADAPTED FROM:
"Jesus: Whoever Believes" from *3:16*
"Jesus: The Resurrection and the Life" from *In the Grip of Grace*
"Jesus: His Special Clothing" from *He Chose the Nails*
"Jesus: The Power of God" from *When Christ Comes*

FOR YOUR JOURNEY ADAPTED FROM:
JOHN
1:1–51 from *3:16*
2:1–25 from *When God Whispers Your Name*
3:1–36 from *He Still Moves Stones*
4:1–54 from *Six Hours One Friday*
5:1–47 from *Come Thirsty*
6:1–71 from *Come Thirsty*
7:1–53 from *Come Thirsty*
8:1–59 from *Six Hours One Friday*
9:1–41 from *Next Door Savior*
10:1–42 from *Cure for the Common Life*
11:1–57 from *God Came Near*
12:1–50 from *A Gentle Thunder*
13:1–38 from *Just Like Jesus*
14:1–31 from *He Chose the Nails*
15:1–25 from *A Gentle Thunder*
15:26—16:33 from *Come Thirsty*
17:1–26 from *Cure for the Common Life*
18:1–27 from *Next Door Savior*
18:28—19:42 from *And the Angels Were Silent*
20:1–31 from *Glory Days*
21:1–25 from *Fearless*